MACMILLAN EXAMS

Ready for
IELTS

Workbook

Sarah Emsden-Bonfanti

Macmillan Education

Between Towns Road, Oxford OX4 3PP

A division of Macmillan Publishers Limited

Companies and representatives throughout the world

ISBN 978-0-2307-3219-3 (+ key edition)

ISBN 978-0-2307-3220-9 (- key edition)

Text © Sarah Emsden-Bonfanti 2010

Design and illustration © Macmillan Publishers Limited 2010

First published 2010

Original design by Andrew Jones

Page make-up by xen. http://www.xen.co.uk

Illustrated by Alan Rowe and Oxford Designers & Illustrators

Cover design by Barbara Mercer

Cover photograph © Getty/Sean Davy

I would like to thank the editors Alison Ramsey, Alison Ross and
Amanda Anderson for their hard work and patience, and the
main author, Sam McCarter, for his guidance throughout this
project. I am also indebted to Debra Farbey, my ESOL students
and the staff of J205, Barnet College, for their encouragement
and advice. I wish to express my gratitude to Richard Acklam for
sharing his pearls of wisdom. But mostly, to my husband Diego
for his love and support, without which none of this would have
been possible.

The publishers would like to thank Sam McCarter and Liz Hunt.

The author and publishers would like to thank the following
for permission to reproduce the following copyright material:
Material from 'All Souls Community Centre Survey' by author
Bolton Council, copyright © Bolton Council, reprinted by
permission of the publisher;

Material from 'Chasing the dream', published in The Economist
07.08.03, copyright © The Economist Newspaper Limited,
London 2003, reprinted by permission of the publisher;

Material from 'Building BRICs of growth' published in The
Economist 05.06.08, copyright © The Economist Newspaper
Limited, London 2008, reprinted by permission of the publisher;

Article 'The Scenic route into Switzerland' copyright ©
eurodestination.com, used with kind permission;

Article 'Orienting Urban Planning to Sustainability in Curitiba,
Brazil' by Kirsteen MacLeod, copyright © ICLEI 2009, reprinted
by permission of the publisher;

Material from 'How our pets keep us healthy' by Rosalind
Ryan, copyright © Rosalind Ryan 2005, first appeared in The
Independent 28.11.05, reprinted by permission of the publisher;

Material from 'How dream of reading someone's' mind may soon
become a reality', by Steve Connor, copyright © Steve Connor
2008,, first appeared in The Independent 06.03.08, reprinted by
permission of the publisher;

Material from 'How to cultivate a greener CV' by Kate Hilpern,
copyright © Kate Hilpern 2008, first appeared in The
Independent 13.11.08, reprinted by permission of the publisher;

Material from 'Melting ice give birth to a strange new world' by
Steve Connor, copyright © Steve Connor 2007, first appeared
in The Independent 26.02.07, reprinted by permission of the
publisher;

Material from 'Renewable energy: Dreams become reality' by
Phil McKenna, copyright Phil McKenna 2008, first appeared in
The New Scientist 08.10.08, reprinted by permission of Reed
Business Information;

Material from 'Cities ear away at Earth's best land' by Anil
Ananthaswamy, copyright © Anil Ananthaswamy 2002, first
appeared in The New Scientist 21.12.02, reprinted by permission
of Reed Business Information;

Material from 'Technology: Seed builds on frozen assets' by Andy
Coghlan, copyright © Andy Coghlan 1994, first appeared in
The New Scientist 11.06.94, reprinted by permission of Reed
Business Information;

Material from 'Psychology and the art of persuasion' by Valerie
Curtis, copyright © Valerie Curtis 2004, first appeared in
The New Scientist 18.12.04, reprinted by permission of Reed
Business Information;

Material from 'The art of healing', copyright © 2006, first
appeared in The New Scientist 22.06.06, reprinted by permission
of Reed Business Information;

Extract and Image from 'How to Grow a Glacier' by Ed Douglas,
copyright © Ed Douglas, first appeared in The New Scientist
02.02.08, reprinted by permission of Reed Business Information;

Adapted material from 'Beijing Olympics: BMX Bikers Search for
Gold on Laoshan Mountain' by Lou Dzierzak, copyright © Lou
Dzierzak 2008, first appeared in Scientific American 04/08/08,
reprinted by permission of the publisher;

Material from 'Mirror, mirror' by Kate Fox, from Social Issue
Research Centre website http://www.sirc.org, reprinted by
permission of the publisher;

Extract from 'How Technology made civilisation possible' from
www.telegraph.co.uk by Telegraph reporter, copyright © 2000,
first appeared in The Daily Telegraph 08.06.2000, reprinted by
permission of the publisher;

Extract from 'Beauty of the Beasts' by David Attenborough,
copyright © David Attenborough 2009, first appeared in The
Daily Telegraph 24.02.09, reprinted by permission of the
publisher;

Material from article 'Touring the Home of the Future' by Momus,
copyright © CondéNast Publications 2007, originally published
in Wired.com 01.02.07, reprinted by permission of the publisher.
All Rights Reserved.

The author and publishers would like to thank the following for
permission to reproduce their photographs:

BRAND X pp30, 60, 64;
Comstock p85;
Corbis pp5,62, 86, 95. Corbis/Bettmann p76, Corbis/
Construction Photography p102, Corbis/Digital Vision p47,
Corbis/Historical Archive p80, Corbis/Tim De Waele p24, Corbis/
Lester Lefkowitz p40;
Creatas p7(bl);
Digital Vision p59(l);
Image Source pp7(tl,cl), 20, 59(r), 93;
Photodisc p43.

Charts reproduced with the kind permission of:
Compete.com p11;
The Economist p114;
New Scientist p51;
Office for National Statistics pp106,107;
Sportbusiness.com p26;
Oildrum.com p42.

Printed and bound in Thailand.

2015   2014   2013

10 9 8 7 6 5 4

Contents

① We are all friends now

Vocabulary 1

Wordlist on page 211 of the coursebook.

Describing people

1 Use the definitions to help you choose an appropriate adjective from the coursebook to complete the grid. When you have finished, you will find that 12 down spells out another adjective to describe a person.

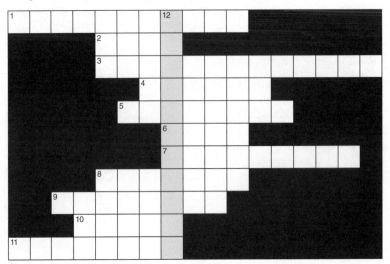

1 Someone who likes exciting activities

2 Someone who can make sensible decisions and give good advice because of their experience and knowledge

3 Someone who puts a lot of effort into their work

4 Someone who enjoys physical activity

5 Someone who likes making things or inventing new ideas

6 Someone who does not lose control of their emotions easily

7 Someone who finds it difficult to be quiet when with other people

8 Someone who has a lot of ideas and enthusiasm for their work

9 Someone who others can depend on

10 Someone who stands by their friends

11 Someone who prefers to be with other people than alone

2 Here is what three students said about people they admire. Complete the sentences with a suitable adjective from the box below. There are two that you will not use.

chatty   adventurous   creative   caring   talented
supportive   hard-working   punctual

a 'I really admire artists of all kinds. As well as being 1 _____ and artistic, they are often very 2 _____ but don't necessarily get recognition for their work.'

b 'I have a lot of respect for nurses. They often need to work long shifts, so they have to be 3 _____ . However, as they look after the most vulnerable people in society, they should also have a 4 _____ nature.'

c 'My grandmother is the person I admire the most. She is always 5 _____ of what I want to do. Even though she worries about me when I go off travelling to new places, she thinks it's good that I'm 6 _____ and encourages me to try new things.'

Reading

IELTS Reading Passage You should spend about 20 minutes on **Questions 1–13**, which are based on the reading passage below.

Questions 1–6

The reading passage has seven sections, **A–G.**

Choose the correct heading for each section from the list of headings below.

List of Headings

i   Why children do not always trust pets

ii   Using pets to help with psychological conditions

iii   The physical and social benefits of having pets

iv   Providing homes for pets in need

v   Choosing the right pet

vi   A statistical analysis of health benefits

vii   How pets can help children

viii   Different types of pet-owner relationships

ix   The origins of a long-lasting relationship

x   Advantages of pets for the sick and those in special homes

Example	Answer
Section A	ix

1   Section **B**

2   Section **C**

3   Section **D**

4   Section **E**

5   Section **F**

6   Section **G**

Man's Best Friend

A   Humans have been keeping pets for almost as long as we have been living in houses. Even in the Greek legend of Odysseus, his dog Argus gets a mention – the faithful hound is the only one who recognizes him after his lengthy voyage.

Most animals were originally brought into households to work, as hunting dogs or using cats to catch mice for example. But the advantages of keeping a pet go far beyond simply using them as labour. Pets are widely accepted as having a beneficial effect on your health, but animals can also have a positive impact on your emotional and mental well-being, too.

B   In 1995 the Australian National People and Pets survey discovered that pet owners visited their doctors less often than their pet-less friends, and were at less risk of suffering heart attacks and strokes. However, the major reason given for pet owners' better physical health was that they are more active than the rest of the population. Dog owners in particular take more recreational walks, which improves their overall fitness levels. But the survey also uncovered the social benefits of having a pet, saying: 'Over 60 per cent of pet owners say that having a pet around when people visit makes it easier to get into conversation and create a friendly atmosphere.'

C   So, does it matter what type of pet you have? Do different pets have different health benefits? Dr McNicholas says it depends what kind of relationship you want to have with your pet. The first is the 'human' type of relationship. This is when pets provide companionship and a supportive role. Dogs or cats would fall into this category. The second is keeping a pet for social reasons. Dog walkers always meet other dog walkers, for example. The third relationship is when your pet is also your hobby – such as keeping exotic animals. In this category, you benefit from the calming effect of watching the animals but also gain from the social aspect of joining clubs or societies.

D The health benefits of pets have become so widely accepted that many animals are now used in hospitals as part of patients' recovery programmes. The charity Pets as Therapy (PaT) has 3,500 dogs and 90 cats currently working for them. The animals make weekly visits to nearly 5,000 hospital wards, residential care homes or special care schools in a bid to boost patients' well-being. The animals may be used to help stroke victims regain the use of their limbs. 'Patients want to stroke the animals so this encourages them to move their arms or hands again,' says Maureen Hennis, chief executive of PaT. Both the PaT dogs and cats are taken into care homes to provide comfort for the residents. Many of them may have given up their own pets before going into homes, so the animals help bring a sense of normality to their lives.

E PaT animals also work with people suffering from depression. 'They can sometimes get through the barriers these patients put up, where humans have failed in the past,' says Maureen. PaT is currently working with a psychologist from Sunderland Royal Hospital treating children with animal phobias. The results so far have been 'very encouraging'. 'We are enabling these children to rejoin the community,' says Maureen. 'They can now walk to school or go to the park when previously they were too frightened to do so.'

F SeeSaw, a bereavement charity set up especially for children, also uses animals to build emotional bridges. Kathy Moore, a counsellor and project co-ordinator for Macmillan Cancer Relief, takes her dog Do-Good with her when she meets children who have a parent or sibling who is dying from a terminal illness. Most children are unwilling to open up to a stranger, but Kathy says Do-Good helps them learn to trust her. 'He can provide such a good way into my first contact with a child,' she says. 'Even if they are a little wary of me, most children can't resist Do-Good – he's got such a great personality and we all go on walks together.'

G Despite the growing body of evidence that pets are beneficial for our health, scientists have not been able to answer one crucial question – are dogs better than cats? Dr McNicholas says it does not matter what type of pet you have, as long as it fits into your lifestyle. 'If you hate long walks but have 'bouncy' dogs that need walking, that is going to push your stress levels way up,' she says. 'You need to do your homework beforehand, so both you and your pet benefit from the relationship. Animals really can give you unconditional love. They don't care if you are having a bad hair day – you can just be yourself.'

Questions 7–10

Complete the sentences below.

Choose **NO MORE THAN THREE WORDS** from the passage for each answer.

7 Walking a dog generally increases people's ....

8 Some owners find that their pets provide both .... and support.

9 PaT uses cats and dogs to .... in a variety of locations.

10 Children can be helped to .... with the use of pets when dealing with bereavement.

Questions 11–13

Do the following statements agree with the information given in the reading passage?

Write:

TRUE	if the statement agrees with the information
FALSE	if the statement contradicts the information
NOT GIVEN	if there no information on this

11 Humans have been keeping pets since people started living in houses.

12 Many patients notice an improvement in their mobility after stroking animals.

13 Children's fear of animals is being successfully overcome in one PaT programme.

Scan the reading passage quickly and find words in the text that mean:

1 a synonym for dog (Section A) _____ (n)

2 done for enjoyment (Section B) _____ (adj)

3 unusual, often from a distant place (Section C) _____ (adj)

4 related to where people live or stay (Section D) _____ (adj)

5 when someone does not want to do something (Section F) _____ (adj)

6 when someone does not trust or is cautious (Section F) _____ (adj)

7 something that has a good effect (Section G) _____ (adj)

Language focus 1

🔍 Grammar reference on page 219 of the coursebook.

Present simple, present continuous and past simple

1 Look at the extracts from the reading passage and underline the main verb. Match the main verb to its usage from the list **a–d** below.

　1 Most animals were originally brought into households to work …

　2 PaT is currently working with a psychologist …

　3 Kathy Moore takes her dog Do-Good with her when she meets children …

　4 … pets are beneficial for our health …

　a The action happens/doesn't happen regularly/routinely.

　b This describes a state rather than an action.

　c The action happened in the past.　　**d** The action is still happening now.

2 Complete the postings left by people looking for friends on the Internet by transforming the verb in brackets into the correct tense. You should also support the reason for your choice by selecting from the list **a–d** in exercise 1. The first one has been done for you as an example.

1 _Hi! I arrived_ (arrive)[c] in Sydney last week so I 2 _____ (look)[ ] for other young overseas students who 3 _____ (want)[ ] to practise their English. I 4 _____ (be)[ ] happy to chat to people online or 5 _____ (meet up)[ ] face-to-face on the weekends when I 6 _____ (not have to)[ ] attend class.

Anyone who 7 _____ (be)[ ] interested in gardening and 8 _____ (want)[ ] to swap tips, please get in touch! I 9 _____ (not use)[ ] the Internet much during the day but I 10 _____ (like)[ ] to go online in the evenings. I 11 _____ (have)[ ] real problems growing tomatoes last year and I 12 _____ (need)[ ] some advice. Thanks!

I 13 _____ (search)[ ] for all music fans from all countries. I 14 _____ (go)[ ] online every night for a couple of hours and 15 _____ (love)[ ] hearing new music from different cultures. My newest friend 16 _____ (be)[ ] from Ghana and 17 _____ (have)[ ] lots of original music. We 18 _____ (listen) [ ] to each others' albums and then 19 _____ (chat)[ ] about it after. We 20 _____ (wait)[ ] for you to join us!

Listening

 1.1 SECTION 1 Questions 1–10

Questions 1–4

Choose the correct letter, **A**, **B** or **C**.

Example

When Julie phones, Mike is

A on his lunch break.

B on his tea break.

C in a meeting.

1 Which type of policy do they choose?

A bronze

B silver

C gold

2 How much does the policy cost for group cover?

A £50

B £20

C £40

3 How will they pay?

A credit card

B debit card

C cash

4 How much did the camera cost?

A $1000

B £1000

C $600

Questions 5–10

Complete the form below.

Write **NO MORE THAN THREE WORDS AND/OR A NUMBER** for each answer.

TRAVEL INSURANCE DETAILS		
Name(s)		Mike Wood
Address	**5**	....
D.O.B.	**6**	....
Emergency contact number	**7**	....
Main policy holder	Julie **8**	....
Date of departure	**9**	....
Date of return	**10**	....

Language focus 2

 Grammar reference on page 219 of the coursebook.

Likes and dislikes

1 Use the table below to complete the sentences using the appropriate form of the verb in brackets. There may be more than one possible answer.

verb (+ object) + -ing	verb (+ object) + infinitive with to	verb + (+ object) -ing / infinitive with to	comparing:
dislike enjoy can't stand	would like would prefer like + object + infinitive with to	like hate love	verb + -ing rather than -ing OR verb + infinitive with to + rather than + infinitive without to

1 I like _____ early on Sunday mornings when it's quiet outside. (get up)

2 My sister hates _____ people as she's slow at typing. (email)

3 I can't stand people _____ loudly on their mobiles on the bus. (talk)

4 I'd prefer _____ a few good friends than many acquaintances. (have)

5 Joanna would like _____ living abroad for a year. (try)

6 He dislikes _____ to the gym. (go)

7 Many people love _____ for others. (cook)

8 Thomas enjoys _____ the centre of attention. (be)

9 Young children like adults _____ with them. (play)

10 Friends who live in different countries often prefer _____ emails rather than _____ on the phone as it's cheaper. (write/speak)

2 Practise expressing your likes and dislikes by using the prompts below. You may need to make the verb negative by adding not.

Example:

      dislike/read   *I dislike reading on the bus as it makes me feel sick.*

1 would prefer/live   _____

2 like/eat   _____

3 enjoy/exercise   _____

4 would like/go   _____

5 hate/listen   _____

6 like people/be   _____

7 can't stand/watch   _____

8 love/swim/sea   _____

9 prefer/rather than   _____

10 dislike people/tell   _____

Vocabulary 2

Wordlist on page 211 of the coursebook.

Verbs of movement

1 Copy the verb forms in the box below into the correct column in the table according to their meaning.

hit a low fall level off remain flat plummet ~~rise~~ soar	
dip fluctuate hit a peak reach a peak drop reach a high	
plunge stabilize be erratic reach the lowest point rocket	
grow increase decrease	

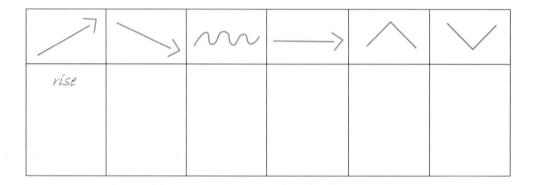

rise					

2 <u>Underline</u> all the verbs that describe an extreme. These cannot be combined with adverbs.

3 Copy the adverbs in the box below into one of the two columns in the table classifying the speed of change.

gradually   quickly   slightly   swiftly   slowly but surely
steadily   drastically   slowly   rapidly   radically

A small change over a longer period	A fast change over a shorter period
gradually	

4 Match the adverbs in exercise 3 to the relevant column in exercise 1.

5 Rewrite these sentences containing noun phrases so that they contain verb + adverb combinations.

Example:

There was a significant rise in the use of social networking sites in 2005.

Usage of social networking sites rose significantly in 2005.

1 The data reveals that the 90s saw a dramatic increase in the number of people using the Internet.

2 There is a steady growth in the popularity of reading newspapers online each year.

3 We are witnessing a gradual decline in the amount of time spent seeing friends face-to-face.

Writing

IELTS Task 1

1 Read the Task 1 question below.

WRITING TASK 1

You should spend about 20 minutes on this task.

The graph below shows the popularity of social networking sites compared to two Internet search engines in the USA from January 2004 to June 2006.

Summarise the information by selecting and reporting the main features, and make comparisons where relevant.

Write at least 150 words.

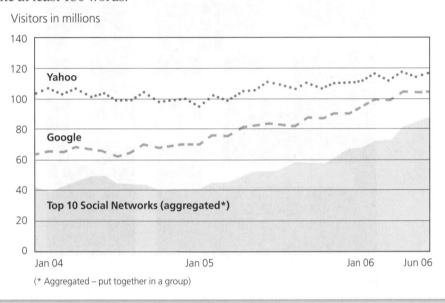

(* Aggregated – put together in a group)

Now complete the model answer by choosing an appropriate form of the verb in brackets.

The graph **1** _____ (illustrate) how often social networking sites were accessed in comparison to the search engines Yahoo and Google over two and a half years ending in June 2006.

It is clear that although visits to both search engines and social networking sites **2** _____ (increase), visits to the latter **3** _____ (grow) at a faster pace. In January 2004, Yahoo **4** _____ (be) by far the most popular site with over 100 million visitors. However, although this figure gradually **5** _____ (rise) to almost 120 million by June 2006, this **6** _____ (be) not a significant increase. Secondly, Google **7** _____ (receive) about half the number of visitors compared to Yahoo in 2004, around 60 million. Its popularity **8** _____ (grow) more rapidly, so that by June 2006 it almost **9** _____ (have) the same number of visitors as Yahoo had two and a half years earlier, an increase of nearly double. Lastly, social networking sites **10** _____ (receive) the least visitors in 2004. In contrast, they **11** _____ (experience) the greatest increase as numbers **12** _____ (soar) from around 40 to over 80 million by the end of the period of study.

2 How is the data arranged in the model answer?

a smallest to largest number or largest to smallest number

b biggest increase to smallest increase or smallest increase to biggest increase

3 Underline the linking words in the model used to compare and contrast data.

② Technology–now and then

Wordlist on page 212 of the coursebook.

Vocabulary 1

Verbs of cause and effect

1 Complete the crossword with a verb from the coursebook that means the same as 1–8 below.

Down

1 to form something in a particular way

2 to become worse

4 to help something develop over time

5 to have a negative effect

Across

3 make someone interested in something

6 to improve something or make it more attractive

7 to succeed in your aim

8 to support something

2 Complete the sentences using the noun form of the verb in brackets.

1 There was a lot of media interest in the new invention, which was part of its _____ (attract).

2 There was a rapid _____ (deteriorate) in the sales of bicycles after the widespread availability of cars.

3 The _____ (promote) of new inventions in the media is the best way of letting people know of their existence.

4 It is important to try and limit the _____ (destroy) done to the environment.

5 The invention of the telephone was one of the greatest _____ (achieve) of its time.

6 The _____ (shape) of our future depends on our actions in the present.

7 New research links the use of technology to the _____ (foster) of knowledge in children.

8 Significant _____ (enhance) have been made to the processing speed of the latest PC.

Listening

IELTS Section 2

👁 **1.2 SECTION 2 Questions 11–20**

Questions 11–15

Choose the correct letter, **A, B** or **C.**

11 Humans have long been using the stars to

    A navigate rivers.

    B draw sea maps.

    C sail long distances.

12 The building constructed by the first Europeans at the observatory was

    A a village.

    B a windmill.

    C a fort.

13 In the cloakroom, people are advised not to leave

    A coats.

    B expensive items.

    C bags.

14 The museum does not allow visitors to stay after

    A 5.30.

    B 5.15.

    C 4.30.

15 The family ticket allows entrance to

    A four adults only.

    B three adults and three children.

    C two adults and two children.

Questions 16–20

Which attraction matches the questions?

Choose **FIVE** answers from the box and write the correct letter, **A–F**, next to questions 16–20.

ATTRACTIONS

A	Powerhouse
B	Soundhouse
C	Discovery Centre
D	Lace Study Centre
E	Vector lab
F	Observatory

16 Which of the tickets gives people a discount? ....

17 Which of the venues is located near the recreation area for children? ....

18 Which part should people visit if they are interested in clothes? ....

19 Which part offers an unusual service for a museum? ....

20 Which place houses all of the attractions mentioned? ....

Reading

You should spend about 20 minutes on **Questions 1–13**, which are based on the reading passage below.

FROM man's first steps to the year '0' was a period like no other in the history of invention. Never again would man's survival be so dependent on his ability to invent ways to solve fundamental problems. And never again would man's technological creativity be the most significant factor in his evolution and the establishing of civilization.

By the time modern man (homo sapiens or 'man-the-wise') appeared, probably somewhere in Africa between 100,000 and 250,000 years ago, his forefathers, the early hominids, had already invented stone tools. It is possible that they had also manufactured crude canoes and shelters. However, it would take many more years and a succession of vital inventions for man to evolve from a primitive, nomadic hunter-gatherer to the highly technologically literate citizen of the time of the Roman Empire.

We like to think that we are currently living through a period when technology has an unparalleled hold on society, but it is nothing compared with that of the ancient world, when invention and technology were the most powerful forces shaping civilization. Throughout the ancient world, technology was the one factor that made all the other changes – social, political and cultural – possible. Without the inventions of ink and papyrus, many of man's ideas would not have spread as fast nor as widely. Without weapons and, later, the wheel, armies would not have conquered new territories as quickly.

The single largest step in early man's social evolution came around 10,000 years ago with the invention of animal husbandry and agriculture. This enabled him to progress from living in nomadic communities to settling in villages and small towns. The progress was brought about by a combination of climatic change and man's invention of more efficient hunting tools, of a means of controlling and utilising fire to clear undergrowth and of ways of building lasting shelters. It led to a massive growth in population, which in turn triggered a further rapid increase in technological innovation.

Most of this change took place in the eastern Mediterranean, where the climate and the annual flooding of fertile soils favoured the development of agriculture and later of cities such as Babylon. By around 6500 BCE, Jericho is believed to have been the largest city in the world, with a population of 2,500.

Four thousand years later, the urban revolution had brought about a momentous cultural transition that in turn generated new needs. These were met by a quantum leap in technological innovation and the establishment of craftsmen and scientists. For the first time, manufacturing became established as man invented ways of making textiles, firing ceramics, producing metalwork and processing foodstuffs. This prompted barter methods to evolve into more sophisticated trading arrangements, culminating in the invention of tokens or early money.

With these technological changes came a corresponding increase in the complexity of the social and political organization of human groups, which in turn necessitated the invention of written language, first to keep track of trading arrangements, then to communicate and record events, processes, philosophies and, of course, inventions.

The history of invention is littered with inventions that had little or no purpose and never caught on, but this was still a period of invention for necessity's sake. It would be some time before an invention would be greeted with questions as to its role – and even longer until Michael Faraday would retort, 'What use is a baby?' when asked what use his dynamo had.

It was also a period when science and technology's symbiotic relationship was reversed. Technology, now often the application of scientific discovery and observation, predated science and in this period was empirical and handed down through the generations. By the time the city states were flowering in the early centuries BCE, scientist-inventors began to emerge. Figures such as Hero, Strato, Ctesibius and Philon used observations and measurements of the physical and natural world to devise inventions. However, they were all minnows when compared with Archimedes. Here was a man of the calibre that the world would not see again until Sir Isaac Newton in the 17th century. The inventor had truly arrived.

Questions 1–7

Do the following statements agree with the information given in the reading passage?

Write:

TRUE	if the statement agrees with the information
FALSE	if the statement contradicts the information
NOT GIVEN	if there is no information on this

1 Man was more creative when civilizations were growing.

2 Before the arrival of modern man there were no tools.

3 Technology nowadays does not drive our society as much as it did in ancient civilizations.

4 If ink and papyrus had not been invented, ideas wouldn't have been disseminated easily.

5 The cultivation of crops and the rearing of animals was by far the biggest achievement of early man.

6 An increase in population led to more advances in the technology of early man.

7 Jericho was the world's first large city.

Questions 8–12

Classify the following events according to whether the reader states that they occurred during

    A the early evolution of nomadic man

    B the early urban period

    C the period of the urban revolution

8 The recording of a wide range of human activity.

9 The possible production of the first boats.

10 Food production as a process.

11 The ability to construct stronger buildings.

12 The use of tokens.

Question 13

Choose the correct letter **A**, **B**, **C** or **D**.

Which of the following is the most suitable title for the reading passage?

 A The importance of science and technology

 B Why man evolved from the apes

 C How technology made civilization possible

 D How philosophers changed the world

Language focus 1

 Grammar reference on page 220 of the coursebook.

Past simple and present perfect

1 Transform the verb in brackets into the correct form of past simple or present perfect. Put it into the active or passive form.

   1 Armies _____ (not be able) to travel long distances before the invention of the wheel.

   2 Man's evolution _____ (be) a long and complicated process.

   3 Sir Isaac Newton _____ (invent) the reflecting telescope in 1672.

   4 Science _____ (teach) in schools now for many years.

   5 Many inventions in the past _____ (have) no particular use at all.

   6 Man _____ (think) that the Earth was flat in early Mesopotamian times.

   7 The discovery of penicillin _____ (help) to end many preventable deaths.

   8 Technology and invention _____ (have) a massive impact on our lives.

2 Look at the following text about how a family's life has changed since they bought a computer. Find and correct the mistakes. The first has been done for you. There are ten more.

> Our lives ~~had~~ *have* changed completely since we bought a computer. I became used to doing everything on it from our weekly shop to contacting friends and family. For example, I speak to my best friend who lives in Vietnam at least once a week for the past year; it's an appointment I don't miss. My wife didn't used it as much as I have, although she was had some classes. However, our children had received the most benefit from being able to use the Internet for their homework. They are getting older now so it's getting more difficult to help. Take last week for example, they have asked me who invent the computer and when. I'm sure I haven't learned such things when I have been at school! By the way, it was a Swiss man called Konrad Zuse, though it wasn't until 1941 that it has become fully functional and ready for programming. Who would have guessed? Not me, that's for sure!

Word building

Qualifying adjectives

1 Read the sentences below and <u>underline</u> the most suitable option.

   1 If you miss a phone call, it's better if it is about something <u>important/unimportant</u>.

   2 I find his music very <u>inspiring/uninspiring</u>.

   3 It can be <u>safe/dangerous</u> if you don't keep a copy of important documents.

   4 If you have a problem, it's better if it's a <u>major/minor</u> one.

   5 Not finding a job can be <u>motivating/demotivating</u>.

   6 Working together is often more <u>constructive/destructive</u> than working alone.

   7 Young people find new technology very <u>appealing/unappealing</u>.

   8 Education teaches us <u>worthless/invaluable</u> skills.

   9 Abstract art is often labelled as <u>ordinary/bizarre</u>.

   10 Leaving parts of the environment untouched is <u>detrimental/beneficial</u> for wildlife.

2 Complete the sentences below using an appropriate adjective from exercise 1. There may be more than one possible answer.

Example:

Early man used basic tools to catch __dangerous__ animals.

1 Ideas written down on paper were _____ for later generations.

2 It's difficult to imagine why some _____ inventions were ever created.

3 Some technologies, like the use of asbestos in buildings, are simply _____ to our health.

4 The thought of not having access to the Internet is _____ to me.

5 By far the most _____ invention of the 19th century was electricity.

6 _____ people sometimes achieve extraordinary things.

7 Criticisms can be very _____ if they are listened to.

8 Past inventors have played a _____ role in shaping our present.

9 It is important for lessons to be _____ so that children want to learn more.

10 Hearing about success stories from the past can be _____ for the young.

Language focus 2

🔍 Grammar reference on page 220 of the coursebook.

Habit in the past

1 Read the sentences below about how a person spent their summers. Decide which of them can use *would* instead of *used to* by adding a tick [✓] if it is possible and a cross if not [✗].

1 My brothers and I used to go to our grandparent's in the summer.

2 They used to have a farm out in the countryside.

3 They used to pick us up at the station.

4 We used to play in their big garden.

5 I used to enjoy chasing rabbits.

6 My grandmother used to cook delicious meals for us every night.

7 My grandfather used to teach us how to fish.

8 I used to hate it when it was time to leave so I used to cry.

Adverbs of frequency

2 Rewrite the sentences about a person's time at school so that the meaning stays the same. Use the adverb and verb given in brackets with *used to* or in the past simple.

Example:

I never missed my favourite TV programme. (always/watch)

I always used to watch/watched my favourite TV programme.

1 I hated science classes. (hardly ever/enjoy)

2 I did my homework. (always/do)

3 I seldom went to sports lessons. (never/attend)

4 I frequently had my lunch outdoors. (often/eat)

5 I didn't spend a lot of time in the library. (seldom/go)

Vocabulary 2

Change the words in the list to the correct form to fill the gaps. An example has been done for you.

a mob wrld :-O

The use of mobile phones has now overtaken the use of ..*traditional*.. landlines. While most people see the benefits of **1** .... in mobile communication, not everyone is happy about their increasing **2** .... For example, some people believe that they intrude on the **3** .... of those who do not wish to listen to other people's conversations while travelling on public transport. However, others complain that if you have one, bosses expect employees to be **4** .... at all times of day and night. In spite of this, their widespread **5** .... and falling cost means that not only are they **6** .... , but increasingly they are seen as a **7** .... item. The **8** .... of mobile technology has also led to functions such as **9** .... text, which saves users the time and energy of putting in letters individually. In addition, a new reduced form of 'text **10** ....' has led to the creation of word forms such as 'l8r' for 'later' and 'BTW' for 'by the way'. Whatever your opinion, the mobile **11** .... looks set to continue.

Example: tradition

1 advancement
2 popular
3 private
4 contact
5 available
6 convenience
7 fashionable
8 sophisticated
9 prediction
10 literate
11 revolve

Writing

IELTS Task 2

1 Read the following Task 2 question and <u>underline</u> the key words and phrases.

> **WRITING TASK 2**
>
> You should spend about 40 minutes on this task.
>
> Write about the following topic:
>
> > *Advances in technology have meant that machines are increasingly used to do jobs that were previously done by humans. The benefits far outweigh the disadvantages.*
> >
> > *To what extent do you agree or disagree?*
>
> Give reasons for your answer and include any relevant examples from your own knowledge or experience.
>
> Write at least 250 words.

2 Decide if each of the following arguments are an advantage (+) or a disadvantage (-). Add some examples of your own.

Argument	Examples
They save us time which we can use to do other things.	
People are becoming less and less active which leads to health problems such as obesity.	
They take jobs away from real people.	
They also create jobs both on the side of inventing and design, to manufacturing and sales.	

3 Read the sample answer below and find the words which are used to introduce a–f below.

 a examples

 b reasons

 c results

 d additional information

 e purpose

 f contrast

We are living in an age of fast-paced development. Thanks to technological advancements, new inventions are constantly being produced that are supposed to help us. However, machines are now often chosen over humans as they are more cost-effective. In spite of this, I completely agree that there are more advantages than disadvantages.

The main argument against using machines is that they take away jobs from humans. Examples include more cash machines and less staff in banks. In factories, fewer people are required as the production line becomes more mechanised. Businesses take these measures because ultimately machines save companies money. In addition, not only do increased technology and mechanization replace jobs in the workplace but also in our daily lives. For instance, in the past we would visit our neighbours and friends, whereas nowadays people either jump in their car or simply pick up the phone. As a result, we have become less active and problems linked to this, such as obesity, are on the increase.

However, it has not all been negative. First of all, we have more free time available from household chores thanks to inventions like washing machines, vacuum cleaners and dishwashers. This means we should have more time available for leisure activities and seeing friends and family. Moreover, technology does not only take jobs away from people but the whole process from design to production and sales actually creates jobs. In order to do these jobs, people need training which leads to more jobs in education and people having more highly specialized careers.

To conclude, although we may do less than in the past, technology has given us the potential to reach new heights that would not have previously been possible. We cannot turn back time so we should concentrate our efforts on ensuring that we all receive a higher level of specialization in the workplace whilst not letting ourselves become less healthy and active.

4 Are the examples used different or the same as yours? Remember, there is never just one right way to answer an essay question.

③ Thrill seekers

Vocabulary 1

Wordlist on page 213 of the coursebook.

Sport

1 Rearrange the letters to complete the collocations referring to sport. Then decide what a person who does this sport is called. An example has been done for you.

		Collocation	Person
1	GXOINB	.... gloves	*a boxer*
2	UNINGRN	.... shoes	....
3	TALLBOOF	a .... pitch	....
4	DADSEL	a horse's	....
5	HIGFSNI	a .... rod	....
6	LOPO	swimming	....
7	FOGL	a .... course	....
8	NENIST	a .... court	....
9	BASCU	.... diving	....
10	TILIGNF	weight	....

2 Decide which extreme sport is being described by these sports enthusiasts.

1
I love coming down the pistes at lightning-fast speed. It's just like skateboarding only up in the mountains.
_____

2
Some people think it's boring, but I love it! When the season's on, I'm glued to the TV watching the world's best car makers and drivers battle it out.
_____

3
I love the thrill of speeding along behind a boat with the wind rushing through my hair. The water spraying in my face from my skis doesn't bother me at all: it adds to the thrill of a real adrenalin rush!
_____

4
It's often mistaken for a violent sport, but that couldn't be further from the truth. It's all about discipline, self-control and balance. There are many types where no contact is made at all. _____

5
My sport is often associated with the rich as it's expensive, but there are ways around that like helping out in the stables. For me, nothing beats the feeling of working together with your stallion to overcome the obstacles in your path. _____

6
I was amazed when I first saw young boys running and jumping off walls like they had springs in their feet, so I decided to give it a go. I'm not as good as the actors and actresses you see in the movies, but my balance has really improved.
_____

Word building

Adjectives ending in *-ing / ed*

1 For sentences 1–8 below, change the verb to an adjective so that the meaning stays the same. Begin your sentences with *I find … + -ing* or *I get/am + -ed …* according to the word in brackets.

Example:

Watching sport on TV bores me. *(get)*   *I get bored watching sport on TV.*

    1 People doing parkour thrills me. (find)

    2 Travelling excites me. (find)

    3 Sports fans annoy me. (get)

    4 Watching circus performers electrifies me. (find)

    5 Extreme sports challenge me. (find)

    6 People doing martial arts fascinates me. (be)

    7 Going for a long run refreshes me. (find)

    8 Exercising every day exhausts me. (get)

2 Change the word in brackets to the appropriate form (noun, verb or adjective).

    1 Hearing about people who have broken world records really .... (motivation) me to push myself to try new things.

    2 Taking part in sport is far more .... (entertainment) than simply watching it.

    3 People of all ages get .... (exciting) about the idea of the Olympics.

    4 I was .... (thrill) to hear my friend is going to trek to Everest Base Camp next year!

    5 Parkour is the extreme sport that .... (fascination) me most.

    6 The new .... (interesting) in extreme sports has led to the creation of many new websites.

    7 I was supposed to try orbing last weekend, but the weather was bad which was really .... (irritate).

    8 My latest .... (challenging) is to try the new extreme sport called 'jumping stilts'.

Listening

IELTS Section 3

1 Before you listen to the recording, listen to the instructions and answer these questions:

    1 How many speakers will you hear?

    2 Will the context be academic or non-academic?

2   ◉ **1.3** Listen and pay attention to the information given at the beginning of the recording about **who** you are listening to and **what** they are talking about. This will help you understand the questions.

SECTION 3 Questions 21–30

Questions 21–22

Choose the correct letter **A**, **B** or **C**.

21 What is Simon worried about?

    A Professor Francisco

    B a headache

    C an essay

22 What does Therese not like about Simon's notes?

    A They're in a list.

    B They're in a spidergram.

    C They're in a spidergraph.

Questions 23–26

Complete the notes below.

Write **NO MORE THAN ONE WORD** for each answer.

Motivation for participating in extreme sports

External influences:

– **23**................................. attention

– **24** modern ....

Internal influences:

– adrenalin rush

– wanting to push themselves – **25** .... need

– element of **26** ....

Questions 27–30

Complete the table below.

Write **NO MORE THAN THREE WORDS AND/OR A NUMBER** for each answer.

Sources for essay		
Author	**Title**	**Content**
Hans German	**27**	research project on about **28** .... in extreme sports
Richard Bell	**29**	overview of thrill seeking
Unknown	**30**	theories and principles

Language focus 1

Grammar reference on page 220 of the coursebook.

Comparison

1 Complete the gaps in the table using the appropriate form of the word shown.

noun	adjective	comparative	superlative
popularity	....	....	....
....	risky	....	....
....	....	easier	....
....	....	....	the most important
difficulty	....	....	....
....	stressful	....	....
....	....	more experienced	....
....	....	....	the most adventurous

2 Correct the mistakes in the following sentences.

1 Skiing is more easy than snowboarding.

2 Bungee jumping is most exciting extreme sport.

3 Skydiving is thrilling than scuba diving.

4 Hot air ballooning is the safe sport in the air.

5 Combat sports are dangerous of all sports.

6 Extreme sports are often least harmful than other addictions.

7 Olympic athletes are the most fit sports people.

8 Kite-boarding is the most new craze in extreme sports.

9 Deep sea fishing is most exciting than lake fishing.

10 To be able to hold their breath for several minutes, free divers need to have the bigger lung capacity.

3 Form sentences from the prompts using comparative nouns with *more*, *less* (for uncountable nouns) or *fewer* (for countable nouns).

Example:

older people/take/risk/the young   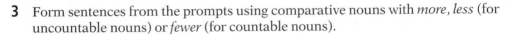 Older people take fewer risks than the young.

1 people/have/difficulty with extreme sports

2 divers/have/fear/drowning/people think

3 boxers/feel/pain/most people

4 children/learn/surf/ease/adults

5 extreme sports/experience/popularity/ever before

6 active people/be/stress/non-active people

7 generally, people/need/adventure/in their lives

8 ballet/require/strength/many people realize

9 men/have/interest/combat sports/women

10 athletes/have/health issues/people who do not exercise

Reading

IELTS Reading Passage You should spend about 20 minutes on **Questions 1–13**, which are based on the reading passage below.

This year's summer games mark the first time bicycle motocross will be held as an Olympic event.

By Lou Dzierzak

A China's first-ever Olympic summer games also marks the first time bicycle motocross (BMX) athletes can go for gold in the world's most prestigious athletic event. Forty-eight BMX cyclists – including four Americans – will bring the sport from its humble dirt track origins in Orange County, California, all the way to the Laoshan Mountain track in Beijing.

B BMX racing is different from other Olympic cycling events in several key ways: the races last less than a minute, the bikes are small and low to the ground, and the racers must wear protective gear over their faces, heads and joints to protect against likely collisions. It introduces an element of 'extreme sports' to the summer games expected to appeal to younger viewers, much the way snowboarding did when it debuted in 1998 at the Nagano, Japan, Winter Olympics, according to Bob Tedesco, managing director of the National Bicycle League in Hilliard, Ohio.

C The sport's long road to Beijing began in 1974 when George Esser founded the National Bicycle League as a nonprofit bicycle motocross sanctioning organization. The first world BMX championships were held in the early 1980s. It wasn't until 2003 that the International Olympic Committee (IOC) decided that BMX would be an official sport in the 2008 Games. 'BMX became an Olympic sport primarily because of the exposure it got on television as part of the ESPN X Games,' says Jay Townley, a cycling industry consultant in Lyndon Station, Wisconsin.

D Unlike the Olympic road and mountain bike races, which take place over dozens of miles and last several hours, a BMX race is a sprint. Not a sprint on a super-smooth track such as the one used for the track cycling competition, but a mad dash across a course that is about 1,148 feet (350 meters) long and 32 feet (10 meters) wide, with three-hairpin turns and four jump-filled straight-aways.

E A BMX racer begins with a standing start and accelerates through the finish line. Riders charge side-by-side down a 26 foot (eight-meter) ramp, angled at a 28-degree slope, to build speed and acceleration of up to 40 miles per hour within the first six seconds of the race. 'Standing up works for acceleration and maneuverability,' says Robert Kahler, senior product manager for GT Bicycles in Madison, Wisconsin. 'You have a very low height to the frame so you can get over the jumps as efficiently as possible.'

F BMX bikes use a single gear throughout the race. Riders use only a rear-wheel brake that is used mostly to avoid riders who have crashed on the course and to stop after crossing the finish line – other types of cycles have a two-brake system that slows both wheels.

G Despite being the world's largest producer of bicycles (59 million units built in 2007) and having the most riders (28 million bikes sold in 2007), according to Bicycle Retailer and Industry News, China will not get a crack at winning the Olympics' first BMX gold medal. The country, which has had a national BMX team since 2003 and won the Asian Championships that year, failed to qualify for the Games.

H But China hopes to win the country's first cycling gold medal in the women's mountain bike race. Team members Ren Chengyuan, 21, and Liu Ying, 23, are ranked third and fourth in the Union Cycliste Internationale (UCI) cross-country world rankings and put China at the top of the international rankings for the first time following the 2007 season.

Questions 1–6

The reading passage has eight paragraphs, **A–H**.

Which paragraph contains the following information?

NB You may use any letter more than once.

 1 the history of how BMX racing became an official Olympic sport

 2 comparisons of how BMX bicycles are different from others

 3 why the new Olympic sport may appeal to a younger crowd

 4 two females who are expected to win medals for their country

 5 a description of the track dimensions for BMX races

 6 two firsts, both for China and the Olympics

Question 7–12

Do the following statements agree with the information given in the reading passage?

Write:

TRUE	if the statement agrees with the information
FALSE	if the statement contradicts the information
NOT GIVEN	if there is no information on this

 7 Most of the motocross cyclists in the Olympics in China do not come from the country where the sport began.

 8 The BMX race is shorter than 60 seconds.

 9 The first BMX championships will be held in 2008.

10 BMX riders easily reach speeds of more than 40 miles an hour.

11 Riders stand on their bikes throughout a BMX race.

12 China sells more bicycle accessories than any other country in the world.

Question 13

Choose the correct letter **A**, **B**, **C** or **D**.

Which of the following is the most suitable title for the reading passage?

 A BMX's first appearance at the Olympics

 B Extreme Sports' Olympiad

 C BMX bikers search for gold

 D The first Olympic cycling event

IELTS Task 1

1   Analyze the following task and then complete the model answer below by choosing the correct option from the alternatives in brackets.

WRITING TASK 1

You should spend around 20 minutes on this task.

Write about the following topic:

> *The bar chart below shows the key reasons for young males watching Formula 1 in March 2007.*
>
> *Summarise the information by selecting and reporting the main features, and make comparisons where relevant.*

Write at least 150 words.

Reasons for following Formula One

March 07

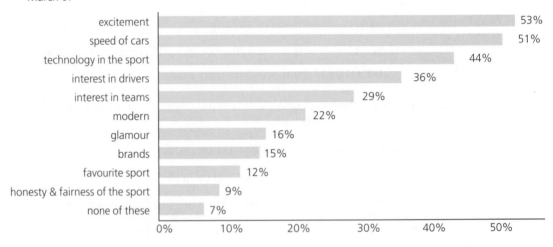

Reason	%
excitement	53%
speed of cars	51%
technology in the sport	44%
interest in drivers	36%
interest in teams	29%
modern	22%
glamour	16%
brands	15%
favourite sport	12%
honesty & fairness of the sport	9%
none of these	7%

The bar chart shows why young men were motivated to watch Formula 1 in March 2007. It is clear that there was a wide variety of responses.

Firstly, the **1** (major/majority) of viewers watched because they found it **2** (excited/exciting), with just **3** (under/over) 50% giving this as a reason. The speed of the cars was the second **4** (least/most) popular response with only 2% **5** (more/less). Forty-four per cent of males watched because they were **6** (interested/interesting) in the technology involved in the sport, whereas only 36% had an interest in the drivers and the competitive nature of the sport. Other reasons, such as the strategies and teamwork used, were nearly half as **7** (popular/popularity) when **8** (comparison/compared) to the excitement felt. Far **9** (less/fewer) people still watched for the visual aspects, such as sport's modern image, glamour and branding, 22%, 16% and 15% respectively. The **10** (most/least) favoured reasons were because it was their favourite sport and only 9% watch for its fairness and honesty.

Only **11** (7%/17%) gave no reason for following F1.

[Words: 164]

2 Complete the checklist below by choosing the appropriate response:

1 Does the introduction copy the title?	YES/NO
2 Is there an overview?	YES/NO
3 Is the answer organized in a logical way?	YES/NO
4 Does the model include specific data?	YES/NO
5 Is information compared/contrasted?	YES/NO
6 Is there much repetition of vocabulary?	YES/NO
7 Is the answer under length?	YES/NO
8 Is 'none of these' a group like the others?	YES/NO

3 Cover the model and write your own response making sure you cover the points in the checklist.

> ## Language focus 2

 Grammar reference on page 221 of the coursebook.

Adjectives with prepositions

1 Rewrite the sentences using the adjective in brackets + a suitable preposition. Make any necessary changes.

Example:

> *I really like snowboarding. (enthusiastic)*
>
> I am enthusiastic about snowboarding.

1 I love swimming. (mad)

2 I hate going to the gym. (keen)

3 I can't run very far. (capable)

4 I love going on long walks. (passionate)

5 I can't stand watching snooker. (bored)

6 I enjoy riding my bicycle. (fond)

7 I love playing football. (fanatical)

8 I don't mind listening to people talk about sport. (indifferent)

2 Underline the two adverbs in *italics* in the sentences below which mean the same and which can both complete the sentences logically.

Example:

> People *never/rarely/hardly* ever buy records.
>
> People ***never/rarely/hardly ever*** buy records.

1 Cats are *usually/rarely/normally* fond of fish.

2 Children are hardly *ever/seldom/usually* keen on vegetables.

3 Footballers are *commonly/never/often* interested in fame.

4 Students are *usually/never/typically* passionate about their field of study.

5 Sports fans are *generally/normally/almost never* mad about sport.

6 Teachers are *always/often/frequently* enthusiastic about grammar.

7 Athletes are *sometimes/occasionally/almost never* capable of breaking records.

8 Teenagers are *almost always/not always/nearly always* fanatical about pop stars.

Global problems and opportunities

Vocabulary 1

Wordlist on page 214 of the coursebook.

General category nouns

1   Write an adjective/noun collocation that could be used to describe the items 1–8 below.
Use the words in the boxes to help you.

sticky golden acute effective adverse momentous controversial festive	opportunity problem solution issue situation occasion event circumstances

1   a national holiday   .a....................................

2   seeing an advert for the perfect job   a....................................

3   being caught in the middle of an argument   a....................................

4   decreasing CO_2 emissions globally   ....

5   losing your job   ....

6   attaining world peace   a....................................

7   a lack of access to clean water   an....................................

8   working together to solve a problem   an....................................

2   Put the following fragments in order and then match them to a situation above.

1   that they/there is/possibility/will reach an agreement/a faint

....[   ]

2   to meet friends/this is/and relatives/opportunity/a good

....[   ]

3   be achieved,/it/a significant/if/it/will be/can/event

....[   ]

4   a serious/is/this/situation/it affects/for those

....[   ]

5   affects/burning/the prospect of/this/survival/our planet's/issue

....[   ]

6   to achieve /the only way/it's/happy with/everyone's/an outcome

....[   ]

7   on someone/ the type of/it's/a profound/have/situation/effect/that can

....[   ]

8   the perfect/it's/opportunity to practise/of persuasion/your skills

....[   ]

Language focus 1

 Grammar reference on page 221 of the coursebook.

Countable and uncountable nouns

1 Decide which nouns are being described. The letter in brackets tells you if it is countable or uncountable (C - countable; U - uncountable).

   1 Rubbish you find on the street. (U) ....

   2 These crimes involve stealing from a person's home. (C) ....

   3 The merchandise a shop sells. (U) ....

   4 We should eat different types of this to stay healthy. (U) ....

   5 People listen to this in order to relax. (U) ....

   6 We make suggestions when we want to give this. (U) ....

   7 Engines and electronic equipment are examples of this. (U) ....

   8 You pack these before you go on holiday. (C)........................

   9 This is the more formal way of referring to what you wear. (U)........................

   10 This fruit is also a colour. (C)........................

2 Find and delete the extra 's/es' in each sentence below.

Example:

Many businesses now demand a lot of works from employees.

work..

   1 Businesses can be carried out anywhere. It just takes the right people to seize opportunities and set up new businesses.

   2 Theatre audiences may be declining generally, but the audiences for the new musical appeared to be extremely large last night.

   3 Public transports like buses and trains will be even better for the environment in future.

   4 An increase in the cost of papers means books and newspapers will become more expensive.

   5 Fruit can go up and down in prices every day.

   6 Entertainments like horror films should be banned.

   7 Discarding electronic goods like refrigerators causes considerable harms to the planet.

   8 Furniture like tables and chairs is often made of woods.

   9 The weathers will be bad at the weekend with violent storms predicted.

   10 Only a little luggages may be taken on planes these days.

IELTS Reading Passage   You should spend about 20 minutes on **Questions 1–13**, which are based on the reading passage below.

Renewable energy: Dreams become reality

WHAT do a small Italian village, a community of millionaires in Oregon and a town in Austria have in common? Nearly all of their electricity needs are supplied by renewable energy. They are by no means the only ones. A growing number of communities are working towards using only electricity generated by renewables.

At the same time, many of the largest cities around the world have set themselves ambitious targets to cut carbon dioxide emissions to less than half present levels in the coming decades, and they will be relying heavily on renewable energy sources to do this. For example, London aims to cut its emissions by 60 per cent of 1990 levels by 2025 with the help of renewables. While no country – except geothermally blessed Iceland – gets all of its electricity from renewables, some resource-rich, sparsely populated countries, including Austria, Sweden and Norway, aim to get between 60 and 90 per cent of their electricity from renewables by 2010.

One of the first towns to adopt a predominantly renewable supply, without compromising on its wealthy residents' modern lifestyle, was Three Rivers in Oregon. 'We have everything – the Internet, satellite TV, a washer and dryer – there is nothing I do without,' says Elaine Budden, who has lived in Three Rivers for 12 years.

Ever since the mid-1980s, when the town's first permanent houses were built, Three Rivers has used solar power. The nearest power lines are several kilometres away and extending the grid would cost hundreds of thousands of dollars. So instead, Three Rivers residents decided to purchase their own photovoltaic panels and battery storage packs. The

panels provide up to 2 kilowatts (kW) of power, enough for 80 to 95 per cent of each household's electricity needs. The rest is supplied by propane or diesel generators.

One community in Italy has got around the intermittent nature of solar power without the help of fossil fuels. In 2002, Varese Ligure, a village of 2,400 people in northern Italy, became the first municipality in Europe to get all its electricity from renewable energy. Instead of relying entirely on one source, it uses a mix of solar, wind and small-scale hydropower. Four wind turbines on a ridge above the village provide 32 megawatts of electricity, 141 solar panels on the roofs of the town hall and the primary school provide 17 kW, and a small hydro station on a nearby river provides an additional 6 kW. Together, these sources now provide more than three times the community's electricity needs.

If renewable energy is going to play a significant role worldwide, however, it will need to be employed on a much larger scale. Gussing, a town of 4,000 in eastern Austria, recently went 100 per cent renewable in electricity production with a highly efficient 8-megawatt biomass gasification plant fuelled by the region's oak trees. By 2010, Gussing plans to use biomass to provide electricity to the rest of the district's 27,000 inhabitants.

Meanwhile, larger communities are also beginning to make the switch. Freiburg, a city of 200,000 in south-west Germany has invested €43 million in photovoltaics in the past 20 years and has set a goal of reducing CO_2 emissions to 25 per cent below 1992 levels by 2010. And if all goes well, Masdar City, a planned development in Abu Dhabi that will be home to 50,000 people, will get all its electricity from the sun, wind and composted food waste when it is completed in 2016.

New Zealand, which like Iceland also relies heavily on geothermal energy and hydropower, now gets 70 per cent of its electricity from renewables and, with the help of additional wind power, aims to increase this figure to 90 per cent by 2025.

From the smallest village to an entire nation, the evidence is already out there that powering our world with renewables can be more than a pipe dream. Now all we need is the investment to make it a reality.

Questions 1–9

Complete the summary using the list of words, **A–Q**, below.

Renewable energy in small communities

While many of the world's largest cities are yet to achieve their **1** .... of reducing their carbon **2** .... , a number of smaller communities have already achieved this as the majority of the electrical **3** .... they use comes from renewables.

One country is **4** .... enough to obtain all its energy needs from environmentally-friendly sources. Others **5** .... to achieve this by 2010, but thanks to having a small **6** .... and the **7** .... of natural resources. Because of the distance from the nearest access to the electricity grid, one town in Oregon already sources most of its energy needs from the **8** .... energy. This was made possible by investing in solar panels and **9** .... for storage.

A community	**B** pretend	**C** geographical
D population	**E** photovoltaic	**F** energy
G assets	**H** solar	**I** resource
J goals	**K** cities	**L** apparatus
M footprint	**N** sun's	**O** hope
P lucky	**Q** way	

Questions 10–13

Do the following statements agree with the claims of the writer in the reading passage?

Write:

YES	if the statement agrees with the claims of the writer
NO	if the statement contradicts the claims of the writer
NOT GIVEN	if it is impossible to say what the writer thinks about this

10 Iceland is not the only place in the world to obtain all of its energy entirely from renewable sources.

11 A European community has an oversupply of electricity from its efforts to stay green.

12 Solar power is often unreliable in colder northern countries.

13 Many new jobs will be created in the field of renewable energy.

Scan the text again and find six pairs of adverbs that modify verbs or adjectives that have the same meaning as 1–6 below.

1 depend on

2 lucky to have an abundant source of 'free energy'

3 very few residents

4 mainly 'non-ending' (energy supply)

5 completely based on

6 very productive/'non-wasting'

Language focus 2

 Grammar reference on page 221 of the coursebook.

Making suggestions

1 Match items 1–8 with their meaning **a–i**. One item has two meanings, a positive one and negative one. Which one is it?

1	overpopulation	**a**	countries losing their cultural differences and becoming the same
2	global warming	**b**	cities spreading out into the countryside
3	urban sprawl	**c**	too many people for the amount of food and resources
4	urbanization	**d**	deserts spreading as the world gets drier and hotter
5	deforestation	**e**	more trade at an international level
6	globalization	**f**	contamination of the of air, water and soil with harmful practices and chemicals
7	pollution	**g**	the heating of the planet caused by pollution
8	desertification	**h**	cutting down of trees, leaving the ground exposed
		i	the movement of people from the countryside to the cities

2 Write a solution to the problems above using the prompts below. Add your own ideas about how we can achieve these things.

Example:

should/encourage/people/have/small/families/by

.We should encourage people to have smaller families by educating them about.
.the dangers of overpopulation, such as lack of food, water and habitable space.

1 need to/educate/people/dangers of overpopulation/by

....

2 can/reduce/number of cars/planet/by

....

3 ought to/enforce/green belts/governments/by/around cities

....

4 people/might/stay/if/countryside

....

5 countries/tropical rainforests/could/be encouraged/not cut down trees/by

....

6 should/educate/young people/cultural roots/by

....

7 can/raise awareness/harm/planet/by

....

8 could/try/change/harmful/farming practices/by

....

Vocabulary 2

Wordlist on page 214 of the coursebook.

Developing ideas by expanding the meaning of adjectives

1 For 1–7 below, circle the word in *italics* which has the same meaning.

1	interesting	*fascinating*	*pleasing*	*boring*
2	motivating	*inviting*	*encouraging*	*maddening*
3	alarming	*frightening*	*grabbing*	*fascinating*
4	worrying	*troubling*	*exciting*	*inspiring*
5	appealing	*stunning*	*inviting*	*demanding*
6	satisfying	*demanding*	*agreeing*	*pleasing*
7	shocking	*stunning*	*nourishing*	*appealing*

2 Complete the sentences below by choosing a word from the box and changing it into an adjective. There may be more than one possible answer.

> frighten   tempt   encourage   attract   stun

1 Obesity is a global problem, but many people find junk food very .... as it is so readily available.

2 It is .... how many people are unaware of the effect of overfishing on the environment. I'm amazed!

3 All this talk of global economic problems isn't very .... when I am trying to find a job!

4 I find the prospect of global warming very .... , and I am trying to be more environmentally friendly these days.

5 He really enjoys big cities and finds the lifestyle very .... I think he wants to move to New York.

3 Decide whether each adjective in *italics* in **1–6** below is suitable. If not, choose an appropriate adjective from exercise 1.

1 Having the chance to experience other cultures is very *appealing*. What makes it attractive is discovering the differences and the similarities.

2 Many major megacities have some shocking social problems, but *satisfying* as they are the cities can be very welcoming.

3 Not knowing about the future could be worrying for some people, but it should be exciting rather than *troubling*.

4 The crime rates in inner cities might be alarming to some people, but surely they are only *encouraging* because of the media focus.

5 Developing new ideas and creating something new is always very *worrying*. It is very pleasing to think one has done something nobody else has achieved.

6 The prospects of finding a better job can be a *motivating* force, but sometimes friends can be encouraging as well.

Writing

IELTS Task 2

1 Look at the following Task 2 question and then answer the questions 1–6 below.

WRITING TASK 2

You should spend about 40 minutes on this task.

Write about the following topic:

> *The migration of people to cities is one of the biggest problems facing the world's cities today.*
>
> *Discuss the main causes. What solutions could be used to tackle the situation?*

Give reasons for your answer and include any relevant examples from your knowledge or experience.

Write at least 250 words.

---

1 What topic do you need to write about?

2 What idea is already suggested in the question?

3 What two things must you write about in your answer?

4 How many words do you need to write?

5 How much time do you have?

6 How many paragraphs should you write?

2 Decide whether each idea a–f below is a cause or a solution. If they are a cause decide whether they are 'push or pull factors', i.e. something that pushes them to leave the countryside or something that attracts them to the city. Then match the causes to the solutions.

a attraction of better job prospects/lack of well-paid jobs

b invest in schools to raise standards

c wider choice of schools available

d better access to medical care

e decentralize big companies by offering incentives to them to move out of cities

f invest in local health care

3 Complete the following model answer by choosing the correct alternative in brackets.

Since the Industrial Revolution, people across the globe have been attracted to the city from the countryside. **1** (Although/However,) this movement has brought benefits for both the cities and its inhabitants, it has also brought many problems. The causes and solutions lie in understanding what pushes people away from the countryside and pulls them to the city.

The biggest attraction is the potential of a better salary and position than they already have, **2** (whereas/nonetheless) there is a lack of prospects if they stay. It can also be beneficial for their children who **3** (would/ought to) have access to a wider choice of schools and the latest technology. If their children receive a good education, then their potential also improves. Lastly, though still linked to the family unit, there are more hospitals and doctors in cities, meaning better access to medical care if anyone gets sick.

Making the countryside more appealing can be done in many ways. Firstly, governments could offer financial incentives to businesses to relocate from the cities to the countryside.

Businesses **4** (should/will) not want to do this if there is no skilled workforce, so investing in schools and education for adults is vital for this to work. Finally, if medical care is improved, people **5** (can/will) be healthier and live for longer, which should lead to a more productive labour force that will then improve the local economy.

In conclusion, the key is to make the countryside more attractive than the city. In order to do this, we need to redress the balance between what is offered in the city and countryside. **6** (Therefore/While) people will be drawn back and should also stop migrating in the first place.

Listening

IELTS Section 4

 1.4 SECTION 4 Questions 31–40

Complete the table below.

Write **NO MORE THAN TWO WORDS** for each answer.

Answers to world problems

Problem	Cause	Solution
pollution of air, **31** .... and	new alternatives to **32** .... practices	**33** .... and respect for nature
34 .... depletion	previous bad **35**	alternatives to fossil fuels such as **36** hydrogen .... in cars
unequal wealth distribution	**37** .... and .... of leaders	solidarity among nations

Questions 38–40

Choose **THREE** letters **A–F**.

Which **THREE** of the following are mentioned as potential obstacles to the solutions?

A new technologies

B unpopular changes

C research and development

D the cost involved

E how laws are made

F financial inequality

5 The future

Language focus 1

 Grammar reference on page 222 of the coursebook.

Ways of looking at the future

1   Use the prompts to write sentences about the future using the tense shown in brackets. Then match each sentence **1–5** to its meaning **a–f**.

Example:

world's population/stabilize (future simple)

...*The world's population will stabilize.*.. [b]

1   I/try/hard/to reduce/carbon emissions (going to)

.... [   ]

2   world's economies/meet/each year/to agree on/policies (present simple)

.... [   ]

3   by 2050/a machine/invent/that/can read/people's minds (future perfect)

.... [   ]

4   near future/most people/live/robots/homes (future continuous)

.... [   ]

5   politicians/meet/Geneva/next week (present continuous)

.... [   ]

a   This is the person's intention.

b   This person is certain that this will happen.

c   This event will have happened sometime before a point in the future.

d   They have planned/arranged to do this.

e   This is a timetabled event.

f   This event will be in progress at a specific point in the future.

2   Complete the news report below by putting the verbs in brackets into a suitable future tense.

Ministers **1** .... (meet) in Paris next week to discuss the environment. This meeting **2** .... (happen) every year but what makes this one different is that for the first time they **3** .... (agree) on how they can reduce the amount of carbon emissions each country produces. It is hoped that by working together the ministers **4** .... (set) realistic targets that all countries can achieve by the year 2050. By this time, more than 70 years **5** .... (pass) since finding out about the damaging effects of global warming. These targets should mean that in the year 2050 the air we **6** .... (breathe) should be cleaner than now. Hopefully, this **7** .... (mean) a better world for all of the world's nations and people.

Vocabulary 1

Wordlist on page 214 of the coursebook.

Adjective/noun collocations

1 Use the collocations below (a–h) to complete the definitions (1–8).

a	An agricultural society
b	The general public
c	A thriving society
d	The governing elite
e	A dominant society
f	A modern civilization
g	An indigenous population
h	An urban population

1 .... refers to the people in control in a country.

2 .... is one that is stronger than others.

3 .... lives off the land.

4 .... is made up of ordinary people in a society.

5 .... does not live and work in rural areas.

6 .... has the earliest historic connections to a region.

7 .... is a group of people who are doing well.

8 .... is related to the contemporary world.

2 Read the titles of the books below (1–8) and then match them to their content using the collocations above (a–h). An example has been done for you.

TITLE	CONTENT
1 21st Century Living	[f] A modern civilization ....
2 The Farmers of the Sahara	[ ] ....
3 World Leaders	[ ] ....
4 Living Together Successfully	[ ] ....
5 The People's Voice	[ ] ....
6 City Dwellers	[ ] ....
7 People in Power	[ ] ....
8 The Aboriginals: Original Inhabitants of Australia	[ ] ....

Listening

IELTS Section 1

1.5 SECTION 1 Questions 1–10

Complete the form below.

Write **NO MORE THAN TWO WORDS AND/OR A NUMBER** for each answer.

Order Form

Example:	*Answer:*
Reason for call:	problems with ...*website*............

Name:	**1**	.... *Freeman*
Title of book:	**2**	....
Author:	*Richard* **3**	....
Type of book:	**4**	....
Price:	**5** £	....
Payment method:	**6**	....
Delivery address:	**7**	........................., *London N22*
Delivery type:	**8**	....
Delivery date:	**9**	....
Delivery instructions: If out leave with a	**10**	....

Word building

Suffixes *-al -ous -ful*

1 Complete the grid with adjectives from the clues below. When you have finished, you will find that 11 down spells out another adjective.

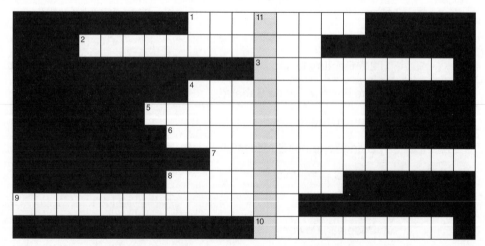

1 a synonym for countrywide

2 the opposite of modern

3 the opposite of safe

4 to do with a place having a large population

5 when something is achieved it is …

6 the opposite of ugly

7 related to land used for farming

8 a place with a lot of room is …

9 to do with modern machinery

10 when something is expensive but not necessary

2 Choose adjectives from exercise 1 to complete the sentences below. Use the space provided in brackets to also write the noun form.

1 People think robots will be very .... in the home of the future. (.....................)

2 Using .... farming methods will help pollute the environment less. (.....................)

3 By the end of the century, fewer .... buildings will have been built in inner city areas as the demand for housing rises. (.....................)

4 Making new friends online can be .... because there's no way of knowing if what they're telling you is the truth. (.....................)

5 Some parts of the globe will always be more .... than others. (.....................)

6 .... developments will change our lives beyond all recognition in the near future. (.....................)

7 Having a very .... house is a dream most people have. (.....................)

8 .... wastelands often dominate the landscape on the outskirts of big cities. (.....................)

Vocabulary 2

Wordlist on page 214 of the coursebook.

Verbs of prediction

1 Match the sentence beginnings 1–6 with the appropriate ending a–f.

1 It is expected that …

2 It is predicted that within the next 50 years a machine that …

3 It is forecast that there could be issues …

4 Sales of computer software are …

5 It is estimated that mobile phone usage …

6 It is anticipated that a larger …

a projected to double in the next ten years.

b proportion of people will be living in urban areas by the end of the century.

c will have grown substantially by the end of the year.

d tracks everyone's movements will have been invented.

e with safeguarding people's privacy.

f unemployment will increase before it starts to decrease.

2 Write your own predictions to complete the sentence beginnings above.

IELTS Reading Passage

You should spend about twenty minutes on **Questions 1–13**, which are based on the reading passage below.

How the dream of reading someone's mind may soon become a reality

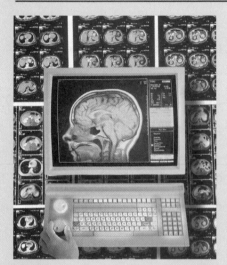

Scientists have built a computer that can 'decode' brain signals and identify photographs people have seen.

The ability to read someone's mind and even to visualize their dreams has come a step closer with a study showing that it is possible to predict accurately what someone is seeing by analyzing their brain activity with a medical scanner. Scientists have built a computer that can 'decode' the brain activity signals from a scanner and match them to photographs of what a person has seen. In the future, they believe the technology will be able to reconstruct scenes being visualized in a person's head – whether real or imaginary.

Tests of the decoder show that it can predict which photograph someone is looking at with an accuracy of up to 90 per cent, although the success rate falls as the total number of photographs being assessed increases. The scientists believe that it might be possible in the near future to adopt the same approach in making a device that can read someone's thoughts, although they warn against doing this surreptitiously or against someone's will. 'It is possible that decoding brain activity could have serious ethical and privacy implications downstream in, say, the 30 to 50-year time frame. It is something I do care about,' said Professor Jack Gallant of the University of California, Berkeley, who led the study published in the journal *Nature*.

The decoder works by analyzing the patterns of activity within the visual centre of the brain, detected by a functional magnetic resonance imaging (fMRI) machine as a person looks at a set of randomly-arranged photographs, one at a time. The decoder then attempts to predict which photograph someone is looking at – from brain activity patterns alone – when the same person is presented with a completely different set of images. 'The image identification problem is analogous to the classic magician's trick, 'pick a card, any card'. In this trick, the magician fans a deck of cards and asks you to pick a card, look at it, and then place it back in the deck. The magician's job is to figure out which card you saw,' said Professor Gallant. Imagine that we begin with a large set of photographs chosen at random. You secretly select just one of these and look at it while we measure your brain activity. Given the set of possible photographs and the measurements of your brain activity, the decoder attempts to identify which specific photograph you saw,' he said.

When volunteers in the study were given a set of 120 photographs, the decoder managed the correct prediction 90 per cent of the time. As the set was expanded to 1,000 images, the prediction rate fell to about 80 per cent. The scientists estimated that even with a set of one billion images – roughly the number of pictures indexed by the internet search engine Google – the decoder would be able to make the correct prediction of what someone saw about 20 per cent of the time. 'In other words, if a person undergoing an fMRI brain scan were to select and view an image at random from the internet, our data suggests that we would be able to use brain activity measurements to identify the precise image that the person saw about once out of every five times,' said Professor Gallant.

The scientists emphasized that at present the decoder can only match pictures seen by a person rather than reconstruct images visualised in a person's head. At this point they can only identify which image was seen when the image was drawn from a known set – reconstruction is currently an unsolved problem, said Professor Gallant. 'However, our data suggests that there might potentially be enough information in brain activity signals measured using fMRI to do this in the future. In fact, so much information is available in these signals that one day it may even be possible to reconstruct the visual contents of dreams or visual imagery,' he said.

Undoubtedly, this device could prove to be one of the most important inventions of the 21st century. Imagine being able to 'see' what a child dreams. It would give us a much deeper understanding of how their psychology develops as they grow up. It could even be used in crime detection to better comprehend a criminal's thought processes and then used to help them rehabilitate so that they do not reoffend. The possiblities are endless.

Questions 1–3

Choose the correct letter **A**, **B**, **C** or **D**.

1 A decoding machine has been invented to

    A read the brain.

    B match the images.

    C predict the future.

    D interpret brain signals.

2 The accuracy of the decoder

    A remains constant as the volume of photographs increases.

    B increases with the volume of photographs.

    C decreases with the volume of photographs.

    D fluctuates as the volume of photographs increases.

3 Scientists predict the decoder could be used to

    A change people's thoughts.

    B read a person's mind.

    C warn the authorities.

    D write a person's will.

Questions 4–6

Answer the questions below.

Write **NO MORE THAN THREE WORDS AND/OR A NUMBER** from the passage for each answer.

4 Besides privacy, what kind of issues does the person who organized the study worry about?

5 At least how many years will it be before mind reading becomes a reality?

6 What was the approximate success rate when tests were carried out with a thousand images?

Questions 7–13

Complete the summary below.

Choose **NO MORE THAN TWO WORDS AND/OR A NUMBER** from the passage for each answer.

HOW THE DECODER WORKS

When a person looks at a collection of **7** ……………………. individual pictures, the decoding machine analyzes the **8** ……………………. of activity in the part of the brain related to vision. Then the machine tries to **9** …………………….which photo the person is viewing. The machine works in a similar way to a magical card **10** ……………………. . Like a magician has to **11** ……………………. out which card was chosen, so does the decoder. The **12** ……………………. rate decreases the more images it has to choose from. Even if the picture was chosen at random from the Internet, **13** ……………………. of brain activity would lead to picking the correct image.

Writing

1 Answer the questions that relate to the graph below. This is the kind of information you will need to include in the exam task that follows.

    1 What does the graph deal with? The past, present or future?

    ………………………………

    2 How much oil was/is/will be used in:

       the past? …………… million tonnes year: ……..

       the present? …………… million tonnes year: ……..

       the future? …………… million tonnes year: ……..

    3 How much gas was/is/will be used in:

       the past? …………… million tonnes year: ……..

       the present? …………… million tonnes year: ……..

       the future? …………… million tonnes year: ……..

    4 How much coal was/is/will be used in:

       the past? …………… million tonnes year: ……..

       the present? …………… million tonnes year: ……..

       the future? …………… million tonnes year: ……..

2 Look at the Task 1 question below and choose the appropriate form of the verb in the model answer.

WRITING TASK 1

You should spend about 20 minutes on this task.

The graph below shows the global production and forecast of fossil fuels.

Summarise the information by selecting and reporting the main features, and make comparisons where relevant.

Write at least 150 words.

Global Fossil Fuel Production and Forecast

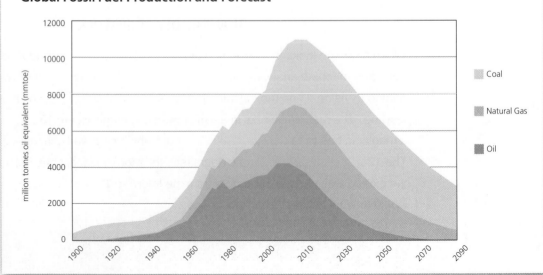

The graph shows the world's past, present and future production of coal, gas and oil. It is clear that if predictions are correct, fossil fuel production **1** *is likely/can* to increase before it **2** *decreased/ decreases*.

5

10

Firstly, ⟨coal production⟩ **3** *is/was* by far the greatest, historically speaking. In the first half of the 20th century, production **4** *will remain/remained* stable at just under approximately 1,000 million tonnes (mts). ⟨This⟩ had increased eightfold by *its* end. Production **5** *be/is* expected to continue growing until it **6** *peak/peaks* around the middle of the 21st century. After this, a gradual decrease is **7** *predict/forecast* so that by the time 2090 arrives, *it* **8** *will have fallen/will be fall* to levels last seen in about 1970, around 3,000 mts. In contrast, natural gas and oil production **9** *was/were* hardly significant until the 1920s. From *this time* up until the present their production **10** *followed/ will follow* a similar pattern to coal's though oil production soon **11** *fell/fall* behind gas'. By 1980, approximately 1,000 more mts of gas **12** *will be/were* produced than oil, peaking at around 7,000 mts by 2030. Conversely, the peak for oil **13** *will be being/will be* both earlier and smaller than both coal and gas at around 4,000 mts by around 2005.

3 Now find all of the reference words in *italics* and draw a line back to the noun they refer to.

Example:

    this (line 6)   ....*coal production (line 1 in paragraph 2)*..............

1 *its* (line 6)   ....

2 *it* (line 7)   ....

3 *it* (line 8)   ....

4 *this time* (line 10)   ....

4 Cover the model answer and write your own version of the answer. Use the checklist from exercise 4, Unit 4 on page 34, to make sure you have covered everything that is necessary and try to use pronouns where possible to avoid repetition.

6 Fruits and seeds

Wordlist on page 216 of the coursebook.

Conservation

1 Unscramble the following verbs and classify them as either positive (+) or negative (–). Then write the noun form.

	VERB (+/–)	NOUN
Example:		
TDRESYO	*destroy (-)*	*destruction*
1 SPREVERE	....	....
2 SCOERVEN	....	....
3 TPOTECR	....	....
4 FDENED	....	....
5 MDOIATEN	....	....
6 ADIREM	....	....
7 PDIAPEARS	....	....

2 Choose the appropriate noun/verb combination from exercise 1 to complete the sentences below. Make any necessary changes. There may be more than one possible answer.

1 Some of the world's most endangered species will .... completely if nothing is done to stop their ....

2 The .... of the world's rainforests will ensure that they are .... for future generations.

3 Nature's best .... are being undermined by policies that leave our environment unable to .... itself from further damage.

4 The .... of the ozone layer has now halted since nations started working together to ensure that it will not be ....

5 Breath-taking views will be .... by future generations who will also hopefully have .... for their ancestors' desire to maintain them.

6 The .... of areas of outstanding natural beauty not only saves wildlife from extinction but also .... plant species too.

7 Nothing spoils a view like a tall building that .... the landscape. We must not allow their .... to invade green spaces in urban areas.

8 In future, people will not only need to wear sun .... when on holiday. If the ozone layer disappears, they will need to .... themselves on a daily basis against the harmful effects of sun radiation.

Reading

IELTS Reading Passage You should spend about 20 minutes on **Questions 1–13**, which are based on the reading passage below.

SEED BANK BUILDS ON FROZEN ASSETS

Exotic fruits growing in a Malaysian garden mark a breakthrough in the technology of preserving seeds. This success may pave the way for botanists to 'bank' the genes of many important tropical plants, the seeds of which have so far proved impossible to preserve.

A The seeds of many economically important tropical species, including rubber, coconut palm, cocoa and coffee, and some from temperate regions, such as oak and chestnut, are described as 'recalcitrant' because they cannot be dried slowly and frozen like 'orthodox' seeds, which can survive in this state for many years. With care, orthodox seeds can be dried until they contain only 5 per cent moisture. So there is little risk that ice will form, disrupting the seed's tissue and killing it.

B Recalcitrant seeds contain so much water that until now they could not be dried enough to risk freezing them. Around 70 per cent of tropical species may produce recalcitrant seeds. To the frustration of botanists and conservationists, the only way to preserve the genetic diversity of these species has been to collect the seeds and grow each succeeding generation. Lack of space makes it difficult to do this on a large scale.

C The jackfruits in Hoong-Fong Chin's garden are the products of the first recalcitrant seeds to be brought back to life after a period in the deepfreeze. 'We are the first to succeed with a truly recalcitrant species,' says Chin, who is based at the Malaysian University of Agriculture in Selangor. 'These are very difficult seeds to handle,' says Chin, 'because they are very variable in moisture content compared with seeds of wheat or barley, for example, which are very uniform.'

D Chin and his colleagues Yue-Luan Hor and Bashkaran Krishnapillay overcame this problem with jackfruit (Artocarpus heterophyllus) by preserving just the embryo, not the entire seed. 'The embryo is more like an orthodox seed, and contains much less moisture than the whole seed,' he says. 'Therefore, it's much more tolerant to cryopreservation.' He says that the trickiest part with jackfruit and other recalcitrant species is locating and extracting the embryo. Even in a seed the size of a coconut the embryo is only a few millimetres long.

E Before freezing the embryos, Chin coated them with a solution of dimethyl sulphoxide and proline, which protects them against cold injury from water in the atmosphere. He then blotted the embryos to remove excess moisture and dried them carefully for one hour. Chin then freezes them slowly, at around 1 degree C per minute until they reach -40°C, before immersing them in liquid nitrogen at -196 °C for permanent storage. He did this in a special freezer which steadily injects drops of liquid nitrogen into the refrigeration chamber. This allows the tissue of the seeds to acclimatise to the fall in temperature before the next drop is added.

F Chin kept the seeds for between one day and a month and found that 60 per cent of them remained viable. 'It's our presumption that they're in suspended animation and in theory they should be able to survive in this state forever.' 'Chin's method is exceptionally important,' says Hugh Pritchard, who works at the seed bank at Wakehurst Place, the country offshoot of the Royal Botanic Gardens, Kew. 'It's the only technique on the horizon that would work for recalcitrant seeds of tremendous economic and ecological value,' he says.

G Pritchard is developing similar techniques for preserving chestnut seeds. 'The difficulties we face are akin to those faced by medical people trying to preserve organs for transplant,' he says. He says that if recalcitrant seeds can be stored, it will be possible to preserve a much greater proportion of the genetic diversity of these species. 'Seed storage is probably the most cost-effective way of preservation because seeds are smaller, so you can preserve a large number in a small volume.' Chin says that he is refining his technique, and has already had some success with rubber. He reports that the jackfruit in his garden seem to have no abnormalities, suggesting that the embryos were unharmed by their spell in the freezer.

Questions 1–4

The reading passage has eight paragraphs, **A–H**.

Which paragraph contains the following information?

1 the quantity of recalcitrant seeds that cannot be dried using traditional methods

2 why using the embryo for the new technique was both advantageous and disadvantageous

3 how long the seeds were kept in a frozen state

4 a reference to similar problems with human organs

Questions 5–8

Do the following statements agree with the information in the reading passage?

Write:

TRUE if the statement agrees with the information

FALSE if the statement contradicts the information

NOT GIVEN if there is no information on this

5 Only tropical species of plants have recalcitrant seeds.

6 Non-recalcitrant seeds can be completely dried out without a problem.

7 The seeds of most cereal crops are much easier to handle.

8 Seeds treated with the new method could be kept indefinitely and still survive.

Questions 9–13

Complete the flow-chart below.

Use **NO MORE THAN TWO WORDS AND/OR A NUMBER** from the passage for each answer.

How to preserve recalcitrant seeds

embryos are **9** ……………………… with a chemical mixture

↓

surplus **10** ……………………… is removed

↓

seeds are dehydrated for **11** ………………………

↓

12 ……………………… frozen at a rate of one centigrade every 60 seconds

↓

indefinite storage is achieved by dipping the seeds in **13** ………………………

Vocabulary 2

Wordlist on page 215 of the coursebook.

Describing sequences

1 Complete the words below describing the stages in a process using the first letter and number of spaces to help you.

BEGINNING	NEXT STAGE	END
1 i_ _ _ _ _ _ _ _	t_ _ _	f_ _ _ _ _ _
2 f_ _ _ _	n_ _ _	
3	a_ s_ _ _ a_	
4	o_ _ _	
5	a_ _ _ _	
6	b_ _ _ _ _	
7	f_ _ _ _ _ _ _ _ t_ _ _	
8	a_ _ _ _ t_ _ _	
9	w_ _ _	
10	w_ _ _ _	

2 Add the appropriate words or phrases from exercise 1 to complete the recipe.

How to make a flourless chocolate cake

Ingredients

225g dark chocolate, chopped
100g unsalted butter
175g icing sugar, sifted
4 large eggs, separated

Method

1 F_ _ _ _ , pre–heat the oven to 180C. T_ _ _ , grease a loose–bottomed 25cm cake tin.

2 A_ _ _ _ t_ _ _ , melt the chocolate and butter together in a heat–proof bowl over a saucepan of boiling water. F_ _ _ _ _ _ _ _ _ _ _ _ , whisk the egg yolks and icing sugar together until they are creamy in a separate bowl. N_ _ _ , fold the melted chocolate into the egg mix.

3 In a clean bowl (and using a clean whisk), whisk the egg whites. O_ _ _ soft peaks form, fold the egg whites gradually into the chocolate mix, in three or four portions.

4 W_ _ _ this is done, pour the mixture into the prepared cake tin and bake at 180°C for about 30 minutes, until the top of the cake is slightly cracked but it is still soft in the middle. B_ _ _ _ _ removing the cake from the tin, allow it to cool on a rack for about half an hour.

5 F_ _ _ _ _ _ , sprinkle with icing sugar, cut and enjoy!

> **Language focus 1**

 Grammar reference on page 222 of the coursebook.

Transitive and intransitive verbs

1 Read the questions below and <u>underline</u> the main verb. Identify whether the verbs are being used transitively [T] or intransitively [I]. Does water freeze in space? [I]

Example:

Does water freeze in space? [I]

1 Can you face the truth even if it hurts? [ ]
2 How do you have a good time? [ ]
3 Why does coffee only grow in tropical places? [ ]
4 Did you collect things when you were younger? [ ]
5 Why does water always flow down? [ ]
6 Does wisdom increase with age? [ ]
7 Would you crush an insect? [ ]
8 Can you pick a ripe melon? [ ]
9 Why do hens lay eggs? [ ]
10 Do you put all of your money in the bank? [ ]
11 Do people really 'fall' in love? [ ]
12 Would you leave your country for another? [ ]
13 Why are the polar caps melting? [ ]
14 Do you always cover your mouth when you cough? [ ]

2 Answer the questions above, guessing when you are not sure. Use full sentences, including a subject and verb as well as an object if the verb is transitive. The first one has been done for you.

Example:

Does water freeze in space? [I] If it isn't heated by the sun, yes.

3 Look at the flow-chart and diagram below. Complete the summary using the verbs from the questions in exercise 1. You will need to use some verbs twice. Then match each sentence to *pictures 1–5*.

Glaciers to order

According to tradition in the Karakoram and Hindu Kush mountains, there are several stages to growing a glacier.

Select a site above 4,500m, facing north-west, surrounded by steep cliffs. Ideally it will be rocky, with ice trapped between small boulders of about 25 centimetres diameter.

Take 300 kilograms of 'female' ice (white, clean and made from snow) and pile it on top of 'male' ice (containing stones and soil).

3

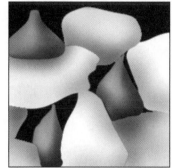

Place gourds of water in the cracks. These will burst when the glacier grows. The contents then freeze and bind together.

4

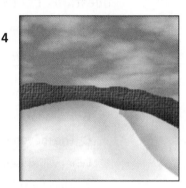

Cover it with charcoal, sawdust, wheat husk, nutshell or pieces of cloth to insulate the new glacier and leave it for approximately four winters.

5

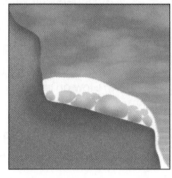

Each season, snowmelt will be trapped by the glacier and refreeze, making it grow. The budding glacier will eventually creep down the hill like a natural glacier.

Summary

First, you should **1** .... a site above 4500 meters that **2** .... north–west and **3** .... rocks with ice trapped in between them [*Picture* ...]. Next, you will need to **4** .... 300 kilograms of 'female' ice (i.e. pure ice without rocks) and **5** .... it on top of the 'male' ice (i.e. with stones and soil) [*Picture* ...]. Then you should **6** .... containers with water into the cracks [*Picture* ...]. These will be **7** .... by the glacier as it **8** .... and help bind the ice together [*Picture* ...]. Finally, you ought to **9** .... the area with charcoal, sawdust or pieces of cloth for insulation and to help **10** .... ice and snow as it **11** .... [*Picture* ...]. It is recommended that you **12** .... it for four winters [*Picture* ...]. As the ice **13** .... in summer and more water **14** .... down the glacier, it **15** .... again each winter which makes it **16** .... [*Picture* ...]. The glacier will then **17** .... in size and move down the mountain as they do naturally [*Picture* ...].

Listening

IELTS Section 2

1.6 SECTION 2 Questions 11–20

Questions 11–16

Choose the correct letter, **A**, **B** or **C**.

11 What will wake people up in the home of the future?

   A Body temperature.

   B The sound of an alarm clock.

   C The movement of the bed.

12 What will shoes be able to do by themselves?

   A Walk faster.

   B Play music.

   C Float on air.

13 What kind of clothes will people be wearing?

   A Clothes that make us more intelligent.

   B Clothes that can interpret how we are feeling.

   C Clothes that are powered by electricity.

14 What can the house do?

   A Control the shower temperature.

   B Turn off the taps.

   C Wash your back.

15 What will the Internet be able to do?

   A Understand when you are worried.

   B Project what's in your fridge.

   C Help find something you've lost.

16 What will the fridge do when people are low on milk?

   A Deliver the milk.

   B Send an email to the shop.

   C Defrost some in the freezer.

Questions 17–20

Label the map below.

Write the correct letter, **A–F**, next to questions 17–20.

The living room of the future

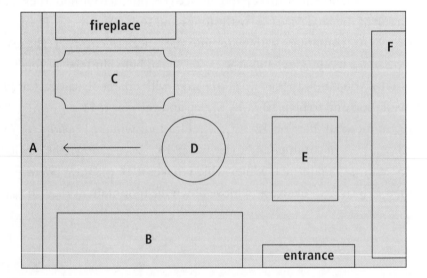

17 television   ....

18 temperature control ....

19 bookcase   ....

20 computer keyboard ....

Writing

IELTS Task 1

1 Look at the following diagram which shows a process. Use the linking words to help you put sentences **a–g** into the correct order.

WRITING TASK 1

You should spend about 20 minutes on this task.

The diagram below shows the stages involved in Ocean Thermal Energy Conversion which uses the temperature difference between deep and surface ocean water to produce electricity.

Summarise the information by selecting and reporting the main features, and make comparisons where relevant.

Write at least 150 words.

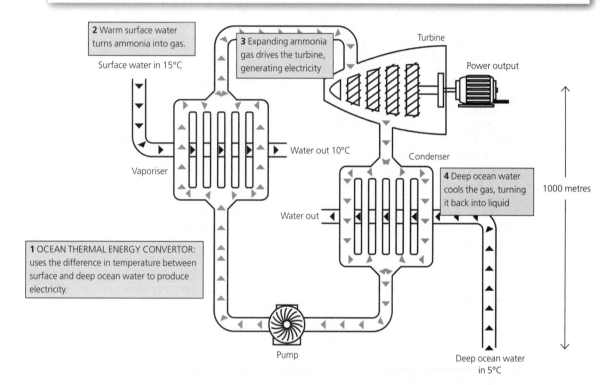

2 Warm surface water turns ammonia into gas.

Surface water in 15°C

3 Expanding ammonia gas drives the turbine, generating electricity

Turbine

Power output

Water out 10°C

Condenser

Vaporiser

4 Deep ocean water cools the gas, turning it back into liquid

1000 metres

Water out

1 OCEAN THERMAL ENERGY CONVERTOR: uses the difference in temperature between surface and deep ocean water to produce electricity.

Pump

Deep ocean water in 5°C

a It is clear that it has the potential to be another clean, renewable energy source as no pollution is generated.

b The diagram shows the technology behind Ocean Thermal Energy Conversion (OTEC) that takes advantage of the differences in temperature of deep and surface sea water to produce electricity.

c When this 'working fluid' boils, the resulting gas creates enough pressure to drive a turbine that generates power.

d First, warm surface water heats a fluid with a low boiling point, such as ammonia or a mixture of ammonia and water.

e In conclusion, the system works just like a conventional power plant where a fuel like coal is burned to create steam.

f While the gas condenses back into a liquid that can be used again, the water is returned to the deep ocean.

g The gas is then cooled by passing it through cold water pumped up from the deep ocean through tubes 1,000 metres long.

2 How many paragraphs would you divide the answer into?

3 Write your own answer to the task.

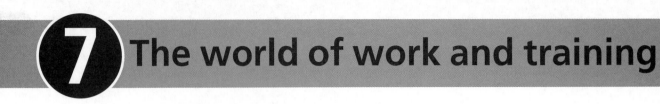

7 The world of work and training

Reading

IELTS Reading Passage You should spend about 20 minutes on **Questions 1–13**, which are based on the reading passage below.

If you want a career in environmental management, it pays to invest in the latest training.

Anyone whose job involves the environment can be sure of one thing: they'll be working in one of the fastest-changing areas of the workplace today. The upshot is that sound training and continuing professional development have never been more important.

But anyone yawning at the very thought of endless dry courses should think again. 'Lots of people turn up to our courses because environmental standards have been bolted onto their job and they've been told to get some training,' says Anne Miller, principal environmental consultant at Woodland Grange training centre. 'Often, they're people who work in health and safety and you can see them thinking, "Oh no, I'm in for a dull day", but they go away on a high, feeling buzzy and saying "What next?" Those already working in the sector, who are updating their knowledge base, say the same.

Contrary to popular belief, training isn't just about the latest legislation, says Miller. 'A greater driver for businesses is reputation. If they look good in terms of what they're doing environmentally, it's good PR. As a result, organizations want their environmental people to go the extra mile. Very often, people phone us afterwards and say, 'Wow, we've just identified tens of thousands of pounds of savings because we're managing our waste or consumption better.' The courses always lead to good news stories.'

Claire Lea, director of membership services at the Institute of Environmental Management and Assessment (IEMA), agrees. 'If, say, someone wants to learn about environmental management systems implementation, they could go on a three-to five-day course and learn about the different components and then go back and talk to management about developing an environmental policy, including setting objectives and targets.'

Some people become interested in a career with an environmental slant after studying an A-level in environmental science or even business studies, where corporate social responsibility is a growing issue. For others, the passion for environmental issues begins at degree level, where again they may study business or alternatively geography, another science or one of the fast-growing number of specific environment-related degrees. The third group of people only really get interested when the topic affects their job.

In terms of the training on offer once you're in work, the breadth is huge-ranging from short half-day courses through to Masters degrees, which can be done part-time or by distance learning. One of the best things about all such courses, says Lea, is that as the learner, you get to influence the syllabus. 'If people demand courses in certain subjects-for example, sustainable procurement-we try to work with training course providers to develop a syllabus.'

The IEMA doesn't actually provide courses, but it works with course providers, approving the best ones. 'The courses we approve are dynamic,' says Lea. 'I think there's a recognition that, especially if you are teaching about legislation, then that teaching could be boring. There has been a push to make sure it isn't, which means being interactive and case study-driven and possibly online. It's about making the subject applicable, rather than looking at every bit of detail.'

Steve Newman, senior environmental consultant for Mouchel, the consulting and business services group, teaches a university environmental impact course as part of his CPD. Newman joined Mouchel after he switched careers and did an MSc in environmental assessment and management, which he completed in 2004. His distinction quickly led to a job in the environmental planning and sustainability division of Mouchel, for whom he now runs teams in Brighton and Haywards Heath. 'One day we could be working on a pipeline project and the next a new dual carriageway or coastal flood defences,' he says.

David Hicks, course manager for the MSc in integrated environmental management at Bath University – which students study via distance learning – says he sees many career changers. 'We've had IT consultants with strong green leanings wanting to convert to environmental consultants and we've had people coming out of the forces wanting an environmental career. Then there are other people who do a job in something like banking, but they want to incorporate environmental issues into their work.'

Richard Ball, senior consultant at Corporate Risk Systems, advises people – whatever their level of training – to consider whether what they learn will be genuinely relevant to a current or future employer. 'The deep green stuff like climatology might sound interesting, but you do need to check if an employer will value it. Try to get a set of skills you can actually use – and if you're starting out, don't forget to accompany it with some practical experience, whether paid or voluntary.'

After Ball's BSc in environmental management, he struggled to find the job he wanted and settled for a purchasing role in the automotive industry. 'But after just six months, they asked if I'd be interested in becoming health, safety and environment adviser,' he says. 'I said yes before a salary was even mentioned.' He was given training through courses and a best-practice programme, through which someone came in once every two weeks to show him how to implement his strategy. It led to him making immediate energy savings of 15 per cent. 'These days, my CPD focuses more on specific subject areas. I love keeping up-to-date with topics. It's so engaging,' he says.

The next step is to get all workers trained up. 'Everyone has a part to play in terms of the environment, from HR to finance to IT to operations,' says Bekir Andrews, London environment manager for Groundwork UK, the training provider. 'Improving environmental performance is no longer just about switching off light-bulbs and recycling your cardboard and paper.'

Questions 1–6

Look at the following people (Questions 1–6) and the list of statements below.

Match each person with the correct statement, **A–H**.

1 Anne Miller

2 Claire Lea

3 Steve Newman

4 David Hicks

5 Richard Ball

6 Bekir Andrews

List of Statements

A The work varies from one day to the next.

B Employees should receive a visit at least every two weeks as part of their training.

C People expect the environmental management training to be boring, but they leave feeling happy.

D The courses that are offered are practical rather than just learning facts.

E Corporate social responsibility is not increasing in importance.

F People move from different professions into jobs connected with the environment.

G All departments in a company need to work together to help the environment.

H How the training received is then applied in businesses.

Questions 7–12

Complete the sentences.

Choose **NO MORE THAN TWO WORDS** from the passage for each answer.

7 People in jobs connected with the environment are currently in one of the .... in the field of work.

8 According to Claire Lea, businesses are more interested in their .... when receiving management training than in being updated on legislation.

9 People choose a career with an .... for three main reasons.

10 Postgraduate degree courses, including Masters, can be studied part-time or via ....

11 The IEMA's job is to liaise with ....

12 It is important that any training done needs to be .... to employers.

Question 13

Choose the correct letter, **A**, **B**, **C** or **D**.

What is the best title for the reading passage?

    A How to cultivate a green career

    B The importance of the going green

    C Working hard in a new way

    D How to choose the right short course

> **Vocabulary 1**

Wordlist on page 215 of the coursebook.

Work

1 Unscramble the jumbled letters that relate to work and training, and then match them to a definition on the right.

1	ALIFIUATCIONQS	_ _ _ _ _ _ _ _ _ _ _ _ _ _	**a** the way someone earns money
2	HDIELLIOOV	_ _ _ _ _ _ _ _ _	**b** work that needs special training or a skill
3	SSOPFEIONR	_ _ _ _ _ _ _ _ _	**c** what you receive when you finish studying
4	PCCOUAIONT	_ _ _ _ _ _ _ _ _	**d** an activity that is done to earn money
5	KOWR	_ _ _ _	**e** another word for job
6	OJB	_ _ _	**f** something you have and you earn money from it
7	LARYSA	_ _ _ _ _ _	**g** a profession you choose and often spend a lot of your life working in
8	ERCARE	_ _ _ _ _ _	**h** what a person receives, usually monthly, for doing their job
9	OBJ/LETTI	_ _ _ / _ _ _ _ _	**i** a move to a higher level, often as a reward for working hard
10	OMITONRPO	_ _ _ _ _ _ _ _	**j** the formal name of your job, often used when filling in forms

2 Complete the statements using one of the items 1–10 in exercise 1 above. You may need to change the form of the word.

1
When I finish studying, I need to make money fast. I'm planning on getting a .... but I don't really care what it is as long as it pays well.

2
Having a .... is really important to me which is why I'm planning to go into teaching, even though it means another full year of study.

3
.... in the future may be very different from what it is nowadays.

4
I'm here at university to obtain better .... so that I can be more specialized in my career.

5
People used to depend on the land for their .... , whereas nowadays they usually depend on companies.

6
When I fill in job applications in the space where you write your .... , I write 'student'. When I finish the course, I will hopefully be able to write 'doctor'.

7
I'm hoping that when I get a job my hard work will be recognized and I will be .... quickly within the company.

8
From looking at numerous job adverts, I've realised that even lower positions can have fancy ....

9
Even though I admire people who choose to do voluntary work, it's not for me. I need a .... to motivate me.

10
I think there's a lot of pressure on us young people to choose a .... from very early on. But I'm just going to find any job when I finish my studies and then decide.

Listening

 **1.7 SECTION 3 Questions 21–30**

Questions 21–25

Choose FIVE letters, **A–H**.

Which **FIVE** things has Sally already done?

A emailed four businesses

B written up results

C contacted three businesses

D started writing the assignment

E read *A Starting Success*

F skimmed a document

G borrowed a book

H researched data

Questions 26–30

Complete the flow-chart below.

Choose **FIVE** answers from the box and choose the correct letter, **A–G**, for questions 26–30.

A beginning

B choices

C document

D language

E opening

F questions

G scales

How to write a questionnaire

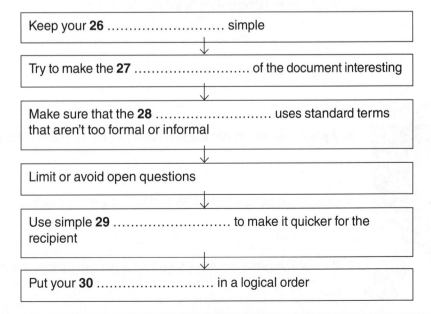

Keep your **26** .... simple

Try to make the **27** .... of the document interesting

Make sure that the **28** .... uses standard terms that aren't too formal or informal

Limit or avoid open questions

Use simple **29** .... to make it quicker for the recipient

Put your **30** .... in a logical order

> Language focus 1

 Grammar reference on page 223 of the coursebook.

Conditionals 1

1 Match the two halves of the sentences. <u>Underline</u> the main verb in each clause and then decide if the first or second conditional is used.

Example:

When I finish university, ⎯⎯⎯⎯⎯⎯⎯ **a** the future would be brighter.

1 Unless governments work together,   **b** we won't breathe cleaner air.

2 If we made the world a fairer place,   **c** we won't be able to solve the world's problems.

3 If people recycled more,   **d** there would be less rubbish.

4 Unless people use their cars less,   **e** *I'll look for a job in environmental policy.*
                                                     (first conditional)

2 Answer the following questions about the future. Give reasons and examples. Use contractions in your answers, as you would in the Speaking test.

Example:

What invention would you like to have in your 'house of the future'?

I'd like to have a musical bed that played me music and rocked me awake gently in the morning.

1 If you could read the future regarding your friends' careers, would you use it to help them?

....

2 How will life be different if we have computer chips containing all the information about our job 'inside us' in the future?

....

3 How long will it be before machines take over the work of humans?

....

4 Will your future grandchildren still be reading books?

....

5 If you could, would you like to have a job that involves working from home?

....

6 How would people feel if they had to study every day as part of their job?

....

7 If it were possible, would people take a business trip to the moon?

....

Vocabulary 2

Wordlist on page 215 of the coursebook.

Collocations

enormous	once-in-a-lifetime	considerable
result in	distinct	outstanding
financial	show	boost	deserves

1 Complete the sentences using a suitable collocation from the box. There may be more than one possible answer.

1 People who go into banking receive .... benefits, like free private health insurance, for example.

2 There are .... advantages to having a rewarding career.

3 It is a .... opportunity that's not to be missed!

4 His latest book was an .... success.

5 Working for a large organization can .... your long-term career prospects.

6 Many entrepreneurs offset the .... disadvantage of not having good qualifications, by using their experience and determination.

7 Many students are incorrectly told by their teachers that they will not succeed and that their efforts will .... failure.

8 Representing your country in the Olympics is an .... achievement.

9 Most students .... considerable improvement while on a course.

10 Everybody .... a second chance.

2 Complete the sentences with a suitable collocation. The first letter of each word has been given.

1 If you *s*................. a chance, it means you do not use it in a sensible way.

2 If you *b*................. your prospects, it means you improve them.

3 If you *s*................. an opportunity, it means that you act quickly and use an opportunity that may not be available later.

4 If something is a *t*................. failure, you can also say it is a complete disaster!

5 Having a limited English vocabulary is a *d*................. disadvantage when you sit the IELTS exam!

6 If you want to *a*................. success in life, you must be prepared to work hard for it.

7 His English showed a *h*................. improvement after spending a year in the USA.

8 If the advantages *o*................. the disadvantages, it means there are more positives than negatives.

Writing

IELTS Task 2

1 Read the Task 2 question below and then answer the following questions:

    1 What is the topic of the essay?

    2 What opinion is put forward that you need to focus on in your answer?

    3 Ultimately, what question do you need to answer?

    4 How can you support your opinion?

    5 How many words do you need to write?

WRITING TASK 2

You should spend about 40 minutes on this task.

Write about the following topic:

> *In the future, written exams will no longer exist. Instead, people will only learn practical skills.*
>
> *To what extent do you agree or disagree with this statement?*

Give reasons for your answer and include any relevant examples from your own knowledge and experience.

Write at least 250 words.

---

2 Read the sample answer below and add the missing punctuation (capital letters, full stops and commas). Then decide where you would separate it into paragraphs.

the future is always uncertain and there is no doubt that we are living in an ever-changing world where little stays the same for long that said education will always be needed though whether this will include exams remains to be seen in my view there will always be a place for exams even if assessment is not exclusively exam-based there is some evidence in the present to substantiate the title's claim traditionally education has centred on academic topics such as language literature and maths which were assessed in exams however more recently colleges and universities now include courses on catering construction and management all requiring more practical skills the best way of assessing these abilities is probably not in a written exam but through coursework and practical assessment on the other hand practical assessment is still a type of exam though its form may be different from in the past in addition there is still a place for traditional skills on these courses for example a chef still needs to be able to do their accounts and a manager still needs to be able to write reports and memos the most efficient way of assessing whether a person has these skills or not is to test them in exam conditions in conclusion advances in education and technology will probably have a major impact on our lives in the future but this does not mean that everything will change completely exams will always have a place in assessment though they will probably not be the only method used

3 Answer the following questions about the sample answer.

    1 Content – does the candidate answer the question fully?

    2 Organization and cohesion – with the corrections, is the answer easy to read?

    3 Range – does the writer use a wide range of vocabulary and grammar?

    4 Accuracy – are there spelling mistakes?

4 Now write your own answer to the question below.

WRITING TASK 2

You should spend about 40 minutes on this task.

Write about the following topic:

> *The most valuable skills learned are practical, rather than the ones we learn while in education.*
>
> *To what extent do you agree or disagree with this statement?*

Give reasons for your answer and include any relevant examples from your own knowledge and experience.

Write at least 250 words.

Vocabulary 1

Wordlist on page 216 of the coursebook.

Nouns relating to places

1 Complete the crossword below using the clues and collocations to help you.

Across

3 I'm a city girl. I grew up in this .... (**13**)

8 They chose an amazing .... for their wedding. (**7**)

9 The house is in a prime .... (**8**)

10 Many people do not live in the same .... they grew up in. (**4**)

11 This is the .... where the Olympic village will be built. (**4**)

Down

1 This shopping area has been made into a pedestrian .... (**4**)

2 Conveniently, there are now two cash machines in the .... (**8**)

4 The ice caps are in the polar .... (**6**)

5 The Lake .... in the north of England is famous for its lakes. (**8**)

6 This area is a natural beauty .... (**4**)

7 This .... makes me frightened! (**5**)

8 We moved out of the city so we could have more .... (**5**)

2 Look at the responses below to the question: 'If you could live anywhere, where would it be?' Choose the correct alternative in *italics*.

> **1**
> Since I love warm weather, rather than very hot or cold, I would live in a *temperate/ tropical* zone.

> **2**
> I love peace and quiet, so somewhere *with lots of open space/in a noisy neighbourhood* would be ideal.

> **3**
> I suffer from claustrophobia, so I hate the feeling of being closed in. Therefore, a house on an *open hillside/wooded hillside* would be perfect for me.

> **4**
> I can't swim but love to watch the power of the sea in action, so a place on a *cliff top/secluded lake* would be amazing.

> **5**
> I'm a big astronomy fan, so I need it to be dark. I'd choose *a wooded hillside/an empty desert* location so I could stargaze every night.

> **6**
> I'm afraid of heights, so anywhere that's not up high, but still has amazing views would be great, like a *rugged mountain/sandy beach*, for example.

3 Now answer the same question.

....

Listening

IELTS Section 4

1.8 SECTION 4 Questions 31–40

Questions 31–40

Complete the notes below.

Write **NO MORE THAN THREE WORDS AND/OR A NUMBER** for each answer.

Impact of Urbanization

The effects of urbanization:

Example: in the U.S.

- **31** only ……………………… of land built on
- loss of **32** ……………………… far larger

Could impact on world **33** ……………………… in future

Research methods:

- a weather **34** ……………………… for clouds was used
- land use divided into **35** ………………………
- data used to calculate the **36**……………………… of all areas

Results:

- urban areas often built on **37** the ………………………
- a second study confirmed that prime land is being converted
- **38** ……………………… of vegetation is lost per annum

The future:

- countries such as **39** ……………………… and ……………………… need to conduct investigations
- stop investing in infrastructure in areas of fertile land
- encourage people to move by giving them **40** ………………………

Reading

IELTS Reading Passage

You should spend about 20 minutes on **Questions 1–13**, which are based on the reading passage below.

Questions 1–7

The reading passage has seven paragraphs, **A–G**.

Choose the correct heading for paragraphs **A–G** from the list of headings below.

Write the correct number, **i–x**, for Questions 1–7.

<table>
<tr><td colspan="2">List of headings</td></tr>
<tr><td>i</td><td>An opportunity to explore a seabed provided by warmer temperatures</td></tr>
<tr><td>ii</td><td>A second, unexpected discovery</td></tr>
<tr><td>iii</td><td>A powerful new submarine</td></tr>
<tr><td>iv</td><td>An overview of an expedition to Antarctica</td></tr>
<tr><td>v</td><td>Flowers and frogs of the deep</td></tr>
<tr><td>vi</td><td>The negative effects of glacial disintegration of the sea floor</td></tr>
<tr><td>vii</td><td>Insight provided into the effect of climate change on the sea ecosystem</td></tr>
<tr><td>viii</td><td>The consequences of the temperature increases on Antarctica</td></tr>
<tr><td>ix</td><td>What the international team of scientists found</td></tr>
<tr><td>x</td><td>Risking everything in Antarctica</td></tr>
</table>

1 Paragraph **A**

2 Paragraph **B**

3 Paragraph **C**

4 Paragraph **D**

5 Paragraph **E**

6 Paragraph **F**

7 Paragraph **G**

Melting ice gives birth to a strange new world

A Herds of sea cucumbers on the move, fields of sea squirts and forests of glass sponges. These were just some of the fantastic sights scientists captured on an underwater expedition to a remote region of Antarctica. Marine biologists made a unique inventory of life forms on a part of the seabed that had been sealed off for thousands of years by massive ice shelves before they suddenly broke up. Waves of colonising plants and animals quickly moved in to exploit the new habitat which had opened up after a region of ice a third of the size of Belgium had disappeared and let in daylight and oxygen. 'This is virgin geography,' said Gauthier Chapelle of the International Polar Foundation in Brussels. 'If we don't find out what this area is like now after the collapse of the shelf, and what species are there, we won't know in 20 years' what has changed, and how global warming has altered the marine ecosystem.'

B More than 50 scientists from 14 countries spent ten weeks making the first comprehensive biological survey of the seabed underneath the Larsen A and Larsen B ice shelves, which disintegrated in 1995 and 2002 respectively. They collected specimens of an estimated 1,000 species, including 15 shrimp-like amphipods that are probably new to science, including one 4-inch specimen that is the biggest of its kind. They also found four species of coral-like organisms called cnidarians, one of which was a new type of sea anemone, found living on the back of a sea snail's shell.

C A remotely controlled submersible took pictures of animals called glass sponges, growing in dense patches in the Larsen A area. By the Larsen B ice-shelf, fast-growing gelatinous sea squirts moved in. 'These ice shelves collapsed due to regional warming,' said Dr Julian Gutt, who led the expedition from the Alfred Wegener Institute in Bremen, Germany. 'For the first time, we have the opportunity to study life in such an area. The break-up of these ice shelves opened up huge, near-pristine portions of the ocean floor, sealed off from above for at least 5,000 years and possibly up to 12,000 years in the case of Larsen B.'

D Another surprise finding was the ability of deep-sea lilies – along with their relatives, the sea cucumbers and sea urchins – to adapt to the relative shallows of the Larsen seabed. Normally, these lilies are found at depths of 2,000 metres. The scientists also saw minke whales and rare beaked whales moving close to the edge of the pack ice that had been exposed by the lost ice shelves, said Dr Meike Scheidat, a German scientist on the team. 'It was surprising how fast such a new habitat was used and colonised by minke whales in considerable densities. They indicate that the ecosystem in the water column changed considerably.'

E One overwhelming conclusion from the expedition was that the marine ecosystem was in a state of flux after the changes in the space of just 10 years. 'The collapse of the Larsen shelves may tell us about impacts of climate-induced changes on marine biodiversity and the functioning of the ecosystem,' Dr Gutt said. 'Until now, scientists have glimpsed life under Antarctica's ice shelves only through drill holes. We were in the unique position to sample wherever we wanted in the marine ecosystem considered one of the least disturbed by humankind anywhere on the planet.'

F The Larsen shelves were attached to the Antarctic peninsula, one of the fastest-warming regions, with temperatures 25C higher than 60 years ago. Since 1974, some 13,500sq km of ice shelves, which are attached to the mainland but float on the sea, have disintegrated in the Antarctic peninsula. Scientists fear more ice-shelf disintegration could lead to the rapid loss of glaciers and ice sheets from the continental mainland, and a consequent rise in global sea levels.

G Dr Gutt said one question the scientists wanted to answer is whether the massive movements of ice was detrimental to the life forms on the seabed. 'During the disintegration of the shelves, many icebergs calved, and the question arises whether grounding icebergs only devastate life at the sea floor or whether such disturbance contributes to a high biodiversity. 'Iceberg disturbance was much more obvious north of the Larsen A and B areas where icebergs typically run aground. At depths of 100 metres, we saw fresh ice scour-marks everywhere and early stages of marine life recolonisation but no mature community. At about 200m, we discovered a mosaic of life in different stages of recolonisation.' The scientists also found small clusters of dead clamshells littering a dark area of the seabed which was probably the site of a mineral-rich 'cold seep', spewing methane and sulphide, which had fertilised the region then petered out and starved the surrounding life-forms.

Questions 8–11

Complete the table below.

Write **NO MORE THAN TWO WORDS** from the passage for each answer.

Types of sea creatures discovered	
Sea creatures	**Found**
New type of **8**	on snail's back
Glass sponges	in **9** .... in Larsen A
Deep sea lilies related to sea cucumber	in **10** .... of Larsen sea floor rather than in deep sea
Dead clams	at about **11** ....

Questions 12 and 13

Choose **TWO** letters, **A–E**.

Which two statements are true about the Larsen shelves since 1974?

A Iceberg changes were more evident to the north of the shelves

B The icebergs refroze and formed new shelves

C The ice shelf disintegration increased the formation of icebergs

D The break up of the ice shelves causes danger to shipping lanes

E A large area of the ice shelves has broken up

Language focus 1

 Grammar reference on page 223 of the coursebook.

Referring in a text

1 Read these sentences which together form a text. Decide which words are being referred to by the <u>underlined</u> pronouns.

   1 The water cycle is one of the most interesting <u>things</u> that I learned about in my geography lessons at school.

   2 My teacher used a cartoon to demonstrate <u>it</u>.

   3 <u>She</u> gave a raindrop a name for <u>this purpose</u>.

   4 <u>It</u> was 'Harry the happy raindrop'.

   5 <u>He</u> travelled on a journey overland, in rivers and the sea.

   6 <u>This</u> wasn't easy.

   7 I still remember <u>her</u>.

   8 <u>She</u> was one of the most enthusiastic teachers I ever had.

2 Choose the correct word in *italics*.

   1 My region is in the south of the country, which is why *this/it* is very hot.

   2 The Amazon rainforest is an area of great importance. *This/It is because this/it contains* so much biodiversity.

   3 For clouds to form, water evaporation usually happens over the ocean. However, *this process/that* can also happen over land from water in lakes, rivers and streams.

   4 The sun rises in the East every day, though the time at which *the rise/it* happens may vary.

   5 Governments keep cutting down trees because *it/this* is a very profitable business.

   6 People move to cities because *they/these* want to find work.

   7 Recycling and using public more than private transport are good ideas. *These measures/That* will help you to reduce your carbon footprint and slow down global warming.

   8 Map reading is a useful skill to have. If you know how to do *it/that* you can find your way about more easily in a new place.

Vocabulary 2

Wordlist on page 216 of the coursebook.

Verbs relating to changes in maps

1 Put the verbs in the box below into the correct column according to their meaning.

convert	tear down	transform	extend	expand
construct	become	pull down	turn into	chop down
develop	knock down	demolish	replace	alter

Verbs that focus on removing structures	Verbs that focus on creating structures

2 Complete the sentences below using the correct form of the verbs in exercise 1. Make sure you use the passive voice where appropriate. There may be more than one answer.

1 The old supermarket was in desperate need of repair. It .... down and then .... with a new one.

2 Last year, the largest house on the street .... into flats.

3 The leisure centre .... , so that it now includes a swimming pool.

4 The derelict land .... into a new sports stadium.

5 The trees .... to allow for extra street lighting.

6 The bank .... beyond all recognition. It's now a public library.

7 A new school .... to accommodate more pupils.

8 To make space for the new developments, the old buildings in the area .... and the whole transport system .... to include high speed links.

> **Writing**

1 Analyze the following Task 1 question and complete the exercises on the model answer.

WRITING TASK 1

You should spend about 20 minutes on this task.

> *The maps below show the changes experienced by Riverside town from 1970 to 2009.*
>
> *Summarise the information by selecting and reporting the main features and make comparisons where necessary.*

Write at least 150 words.

Map of Riverside Town 1970

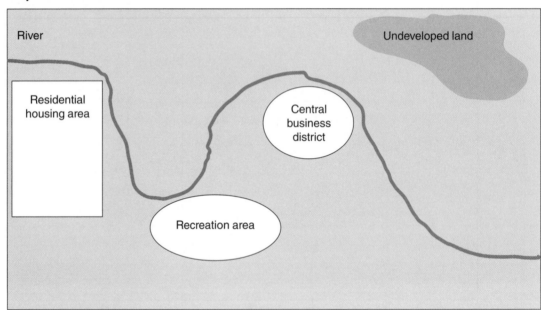

Map of Riverside Town 2009

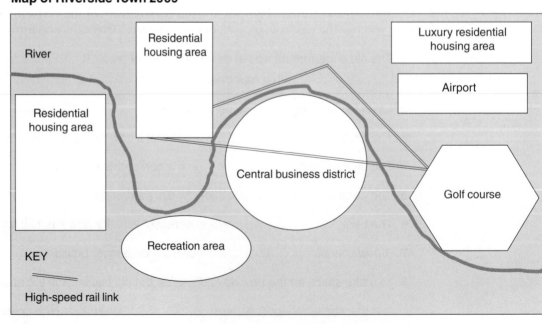

2 Read the first part of the model answer and choose the correct alternative.

> The maps **1** illustrates/illustrate the developments in Riverside town over a thirty-nine year period. It is clear **2** this/that there has been considerable investment in urban planning and infrastructure during this time.
>
> In 1970, Riverside **3** is/was a relatively small town with construction only on the land **4** in the south/to the south of the river. There was one main residential area to the west with a comparatively large recreational area near it. The central business district (CBD) was also small and the area **5** in the north/north of the river was completely undeveloped providing green open space for its residents.

3 Now put the rest of the model answer in order using the referring words and linking words to help you.

a Furthermore, there is a new golf course to the east of the town, just north of the river.

b In contrast, the old central business district maintains its central location but has almost doubled in size.

c However, by the year 2009, the town's residential areas tripled.

d Finally, the last remaining enclosure to the south of the river that has not changed is the recreational area though it now looks small by comparison.

e Noticeably, these new facilities and transport links do not extend to the original residential area.

f These are now connected to the new transport links which were also improved to include both a high-speed rail link and airport.

g The new residential districts, one of which is luxury apartments, were built north of the river.

4 Write your own answer to the question.

(9) What is beauty?

Vocabulary 1

Wordlist on page 215 of the coursebook.

Beauty

1   The adjectives below can be used to describe objects or how people feel. Tick the appropriate column in each case.

	Object	People's feelings
ancient	✓	
beautiful		
dazzling		
ecstatic		
emotional		
evocative		
humbling		
impressive		
magnificent		
majestic		
melancholic		
nostalgic		
overawed		
overjoyed		
overwhelmed		
spacious		
thoughtful		

2   Choose at least one adjective from exercise 1 to describe how the speaker feels in each case below.

1   'My new flat is amazing! It's much bigger than my last place and the view also reminds me of my hometown so it makes me feel homesick, but in a good way.'
....

2   'I am happier than I could ever imagine to find this job, mainly because I didn't expect to be successful at the interview. Working in such a magnificent and famous building made me feel proud and modest at the same time.' ....

3   'Listening to soul music always makes me feel sad. I find the words really reminiscent of the time I lost my first true love.' ....

4   'My colleagues were really kind when I was sick. They sent me some beautiful flowers and messages of support. Their generosity left me so touched I just couldn't stop thinking about it.' ....

5   'Our architecture teacher did such a brilliant job that all of the students passed with flying colours. She is both strict and intimidating, so I was a bit scared at first. '
....

6   'The setting for my best friend's wedding was a magnificent old castle.'
....

68

Listening

IELTS Section 3

⊙ 2.1 SECTION 3 Questions 21–30

Questions 21–25

Choose the correct letter, **A**, **B** or **C**.

21 Which college does Chris suggest would be best?

   A Leeds Conservatory of Contemporary Music

   B The Henry Music Institute

   C The Academy in London

22 What entry requirements are common to all the colleges?

   A an audition

   B an essay

   C an interview

23 How much does the course at Leeds Conservatory of Contemporary Music cost?

   A £6,000 a year

   B £7,000 a year

   C £8,000 a year

24 What other expenses are payable to the colleges?

   A application fee

   B insurance

   C train fare

25 When is the deadline for Leeds Conservatory of Contemporary Music?

   A January 9th

   B January 19th

   C January 30th

Questions 26–30

Which facilities do the colleges have?

Choose **FIVE** answers from the box and write the correct letter, **A–G**, next to questions 26–30.

Facilities
A large gardens
B multiple sites
C practice rooms
D recording studio
E research facility
F student canteen
G technology suite

Colleges

26 Northdown College   ....

27 The Academy in London   ....

28 Leeds Conservatory of Contemporary Music   ....

29 The Henry Music Institute   ....

30 The James Academy of Music   ....

Reading

You should spend about **20** minutes on **Questions 1–13**, which are based on the reading passage below.

Mirror, mirror

We are all more obsessed with our appearance than we like to admit. But this is not an indication of 'vanity'. Vanity means conceit, excessive pride in one's appearance. Concern about appearance is quite normal and understandable.

Attractive people have distinct advantages in our society. Studies show that attractive children are more popular, both with classmates and teachers. Teachers give higher evaluations to the work of attractive children and have higher expectations of them (which has been shown to improve performance). Attractive applicants have a better chance of getting jobs, and of receiving higher salaries. In court, attractive people are found guilty less often. When found guilty, they receive less severe sentences. The 'bias for beauty' operates in almost all social situations – all experiments show we react more favourably to physically attractive people.

We also believe in the 'what is beautiful is good' stereotype – an irrational but deep-seated belief that physically attractive people possess other desirable characteristics such as intelligence, competence, social skills, confidence – even moral virtue. (The good fairy/princess is always beautiful; the wicked stepmother is always ugly.) Therefore, it is not surprising that physical attractiveness is of overwhelming importance to us.

Concern with appearance is not just an aberration of Modern Western culture. Every period of history has had its own standards of what is and is not beautiful, and every contemporary society has its own distinctive concept of the ideal physical attributes. In the 19th century being beautiful meant wearing a corset – causing breathing and digestive problems. Now we try to diet and exercise ourselves into the fashionable shape – often with even more serious consequences.

Although we resemble our ancestors and other cultures in our concern about appearance, there is a difference in degree of concern. Advances in technology and in particular the rise of the mass media have caused normal concerns about how we look to become obsessions. Thanks to the media, we have become accustomed to extremely rigid and uniform standards of beauty. TV, billboards, magazines, etc. mean that we see 'beautiful people' all the time, more often than members of our own family, making exceptional good looks seem real, normal and attainable. Standards of beauty have in fact become harder and harder to attain, particularly for women.

Even very attractive people may not be looking in the mirror out of 'vanity', but out of insecurity. We forget that there are disadvantages to being attractive: attractive people are under much greater pressure to maintain their appearance. Also, studies show that attractive people don't benefit from the 'bias for beauty' in terms of self-esteem. They often don't trust praise of their work or talents, believing positive evaluations to be influenced by their appearance.

What people see and how they react to their reflection in a mirror will vary according to: sex, age, ethnic group, sexual orientation, mood, eating disorders, what they've been watching on TV, what magazines they read, whether they're married or single, what kind of childhood they had, whether they take part in sports, what phase of the menstrual cycle they're in, whether they are pregnant, where they've been shopping – and even what they had for lunch.

If you were a dog or a cat or a horse, you wouldn't realise that the image was a reflection of yourself. Most animals in this situation think that they are face to face with another member of their species. The exception is the great apes – chimps, gorillas and orang-utans are capable of recognising themselves in the mirror – and of course, us. What's interesting is what the apes do when presented with a mirror: they use mirrors to groom themselves, pick food out of their teeth and make faces at themselves for entertainment – i.e. more or less the same reactions as us.

All research to date on body image shows that women are much more critical of their appearance than men – much less likely to admire what they see in the mirror. Up to 8 out of 10 women will be dissatisfied with their reflection, and more than half may see a distorted image. Men looking in the mirror are more likely to be either pleased with what they see or indifferent. Research shows that men generally have a much more positive body-image than women – if anything, they may tend to over-estimate their attractiveness. Some men looking in the mirror may literally not see the flaws in their appearance.

Why are women so much more self-critical than men? Because women are judged on their appearance more than men, and standards of female beauty are considerably higher and more inflexible. Women are continually bombarded with images of the 'ideal' face and figure. Also, most women are trying to achieve the impossible: standards of female beauty have in fact become progressively more unrealistic during the 20th century. In 1917, the physically perfect woman was about 5ft 4in tall and weighed nearly 10 stone. Even 25 years ago, top models and beauty queens weighed only 8% less than the average woman, now they weigh 23% less. The current media ideal for women is achievable by less than 5% of the female population – and that's just in terms of weight and size. If you want the ideal shape, face, etc, it's probably more like 1%.

Questions 1–6

Complete the sentences below.

Choose **NO MORE THAN THREE WORDS** from the passage for each answer.

1 Vain people are too proud of their ....

2 In nearly all social contexts, tests have proven that a .... is at work.

3 The belief that being beautiful is equal to being 'a good person' is

....

4 People's idea of the .... depends on the period they live in.

5 While it is normal for everybody to worry about how they look, the
.... has changed so that it now borders on fixation.

6 Due to the media, people are now used to very .... principles of
what is beautiful.

Questions 7–11

Do the following statements agree with the views of the writer in the reading passage?

Write:

> **YES**   if the statement agrees with the views of the writer
>
> **NO**   if the statement contradicts the views of the writer
>
> **NOT GIVEN**   if it is impossible to say what the writer thinks about this

7 The only reason that good-looking people look in the mirror is because they are vain.

8 All primates imitate typically human behaviour when looking in a mirror.

9 Only a minority of women look in the mirror and see an image that is not a true
reflection of themselves.

10 It has been scientifically proven that, of the two sexes, males are more confident about
their appearance.

11 It is more common for a man to miss imperfections in the way he looks than a woman.

Questions 12 and13

Choose **TWO** letters, **A–E**.

Which **TWO** reasons for women being more self-conscious about their appearance than
men are mentioned by the writer of the passage?

A Increasingly unrealistic 20th century developments

B An increase in women's weight

C A tendency to be more insecure

D The influence of TV and magazines

E Expectations are greater and more rigid

> **Word building**

Prefixes *under-* and *over-*

1 Make adjectives and verbs using the prefixes *over-* and *under-* with the words below.

    1 rate

    2 estimate

    3 take

    4 state

    5 price

    6 value

    7 run

    8 awe

2 Are the adjectives and verbs in exercise 1 positive (+), negative (-) or neutral (o). Decide which adjective can have both a positive and negative meaning.

3 Reorder the fragments below to make sentences. Note in each list there is one extra word that you cannot use.

    1 first saw it/She was completely/of the landscape/overawed/when she overestimated/by the beauty

    ....

    2 very appealing,/blatantly overpriced/the undervalued car/Even though/was/it was

    ....

    3 tourist attractions in the city/Attendances/understated/at the Museum of Modern Art/ have recently/all the other major/overtaken

    ....

    4 of beautiful/on people's/the impact/surroundings/well-being/It's easy/overawed/ to underestimate

    ....

    5 her wealth is understated as/clothes/overstated/she doesn't/Although she's a wealthy lady,/wear flashy

    ....

    6 overtaken/architecturally that/with tourists/all year round/it is overrun/My home village/ is so attractive

    ....

    7 The actors and actresses/undervalued/over their pay,/which made/were on strike/ them feel/overvalued

    ....

    8 the film/I expected/to be better/overrated reviews/it received/overrun/than the

    ....

Language focus 1

 Grammar reference on page 224 of the coursebook.

Modal verbs for evaluating

1 Read the two sentences below. Decide which one is about the past, and which about the present. Use the examples to complete the rules on how to form them.

   i 'I <u>should have made</u> a back–up of my art work, because I lost everything when the computer crashed.' ....

   ii 'I <u>must buy</u> a new computer as soon as possible.' ....

VERB FORM

Talking about the past:

modal + _____ + _____

Talking about the present/future:

_____ + infinitive verb (without/*to*)

2 Analyze the meaning of the sentences i and ii above and tick [✓] the statements that are true and cross [✗] the ones that are not.

MEANING

Talking about the present/future:

   a This speaker wants to do this, but hasn't done it yet.

   b This speaker has already done this, but we don't know when.

Talking about the past:

   a This speaker mentions an action that actually happened.

   b The speaker says this action didn't happen, but thinks the action needed to be taken.

3 Practise evaluating the situations below, using the modal and the verb given in brackets. Add a reason to explain each one.

   Example:

     The air pollution in the historical areas of your city is bad. It is caused by the number of cars.   (should limit)

     They should limit the number of cars on the road so the air will be cleaner.

   1 They have closed down your local shop.   (could keep open)

     ....

   2 Your friend's pottery exam is tomorrow. She is tired.   (ought to go)

     ....

   3 Your teacher gave you too much art homework yesterday. You tell them today. (should give)

     ....

   4 You disagree with predictions about a football match.   (might win)

     ....

   5 Tomorrow is a national holiday. You want to go to a place of natural beauty for a picnic. You suggest it to your family.   (could visit)

     ....

   6 Sydney was voted the most beautiful city in the world. You think it should be your city. (would vote)

     ....

Writing

IELTS Task 2

1 Analyze the following Task 2 question. <u>Underline</u> the key words and phrases.

WRITING TASK 2

You should spend about 40 minutes on this task.

Write about the following topic:

> *Advertising is made more and more appealing to the general public nowadays. However beautiful it is, it serves no useful purpose and encourages people to spend too much money on things they do not really need.*
>
> *To what extent do you agree or disagree?*

Give reasons for your answer and include any relevant examples from your own knowledge and experience.

Write at least 250 words.

---

2 Look at the first statement. Do you agree that:

– advertising is everywhere nowadays? Yes/No

– it has no useful purpose? Yes/No

– it encourages people to buy things they don't need? Yes/No

– spending <u>any</u> money on advertising is a waste? Yes/No

– it is a good idea to spend more money on the other things? Yes/No

3 Read the model answer below and <u>underline</u> the words/phrases that show effect. The first two are done for you.

We live in a consumer age and this often means we are encouraged to buy things we do not really need just because they look attractive in advertisements. However, to say that advertising plays no useful role is simply not true. Although spending more money on education is a good idea, it should not be at the expense of advertising.

There are arguments in favour of reducing the amount of advertising. Many people find it annoying and feel bombarded <u>as they are everywhere</u> nowadays. This in turn leads them to deliberately avoid them, by switching TV channels, for example. In addition, advertising such as leaflets simply end up on the streets as litter, which is not pleasing to the eye or good for the environment. All of these arguments support the case for reducing the amount of advertising.

On the other hand, there are many arguments in favour of keeping advertising. Firstly, without it most people would not know when a new product or invention was available. This would impact on people's lives and mean that we would not be able to take advantage of new time-saving devices. Take the washing machine, for example. If most people had never heard of one and were still washing their clothes by hand, they would work less, which would impact on society's progress. Secondly, people employed in the advertising industry would lose their jobs, and this would not stop there. Manufacturing industries would also suffer from not selling as many products, and therefore, would employ fewer people who would pay fewer taxes. Everyone would suffer.

To sum up, while there are obvious advantages to controlling the amount of advertising. Life without it would be unrecognisable from our present. There will always be more worthy causes, such as education, but without advertising, education would not be necessary as there would be so few jobs that require one.

4 Answer the question below.

WRITING TASK 2

You should spend about 40 minutes on this task.

Write about the following topic:

> *Too much money is spent by individuals and governments on making themselves and the areas they live in look beautiful. This is wasteful and it has no useful purpose.*
>
> *Instead, the money should be spent on improving individuals' health.*
>
> *Do you agree or disagree with this opinion?*

Give reasons for your answer and include any relevant examples from your own knowledge and experience.

Write at least 250 words.

⑩ Is it art?

Listening

👁 **2.2 SECTION 4 Questions 31–40**

Questions 31–35

Complete the sentences below.

Write **NO MORE THAN TWO WORDS AND/OR A NUMBER** for each answer.

The health benefits of art and music

31 According to the speaker, art and music can benefit patients' emotional, ... and physical well-being.

32 Florence Nightingale first noted the improvements in the year ....

33 The results of many studies did not prove a link between health and art as they were rarely ....

34 The American study looked at the effects of architecture on patients' ....

35 The patients who were in a ward with a .... were not in hospital for as long and needed less medication.

Questions 36–40

Complete the table below.

Write **NO MORE THAN THREE WORDS** for each answer.

Recent Research Projects

Type of patient	Type of art/music	Effect on patients	Other improvements
Unborn babies	**36**	heart rate increased	mothers felt relaxed
Cancer patients	**37**	**38**	improvements in well-being
Hip replacement (elderly)	**39**	eased anxiety	**40** staff ....

Vocabulary 1

Wordlist on page 217 of the coursebook.

Art

1 Look at the list of art forms below and cross out the word(s) in each list which is/are not associated with them. Then add it to the list to which it belongs. One list has two words that need to be crossed out.

Example:

> newspaper journalist/~~composer~~/editor/printer/contributor/reader/ *columnist*

1 play   actor/actress/conductor/lead role/director/producer/ ....

2 painting   artist/easel/canvas/columnist/portrait/stone/ ....

3 book   novelist/writer/author/landscape/editor/critic/ ....

4 symphony   composer/musician/reader/movement/ ....

5 sculpture   sculptor/artist/carving/mould/lens/marble/ ....

6 photograph   photographer/digital/film/portrait/choreographer/ ....

7 ballet   dancer/composer/musician/ballerina/script writer/ ....

8 film   actor/actress/director/star/producer/playwright/ ....

2 Decide which of the people listed in exercise 1 would say the statements below.

Example:

> 'My dream is to play the lead role on the stage at London's West End.' *actor/actress*

1
It can be quite nerve-racking standing up there in front of all those people; even if I have my back to the ones I don't know. All eyes are on you!
....

2
Getting ordinary people to relax is a challenge. However, once they've got a nice pose and expression, other imperfections can be 'ironed out' digitally. ....

3
In my opinion, it's the hardest job on the set. But someone needs to take charge of the finances and other important decisions, or we'd never finish a project.
....

4
Working with models can be quite challenging, which is why I prefer still life subjects as I can go back to them for days or even weeks if I need to. A model, would definitely complain about sitting for so long!
....

5
Girls sometimes want to be one when they are small but the training regime is actually one of the hardest in terms of its physical demands. My job requires early starts, long practice sessions and lots of injuries. The result though is beautiful and graceful, I'm sure you'll agree if you watch. ....

6
I love working with my hands and getting them dirty to get the best out of the material I'm working with. I often have a vision, but I'm never exactly sure what the end product will look like. The most important thing for me is that people stop and enjoy my work when they are passing it.
....

7
People in my industry often mistakenly think my job is easy. Reading through several books, articles and other publications a week takes time, and I have to be brutally honest as people buy my recommendations.
....

Language focus 1

 Grammar reference on page 224 of the coursebook.

Defining and non-defining relative clauses

1 Combine the sentences using a non-defining relative clause. The first two sentences have words underlined to help you. Remember that you will need to use (a) comma(s)!

Example:

Classical music helps me relax. I listen to it in the evenings.

Classical music, which I listen to in the evenings, helps me relax.

1 Studying English grammar can be difficult. It is often frustrating.

....

2 Shakespeare wrote Romeo and Juliet. It's my favourite play.

....

3 This is Peter. He'll be working with us on the next project.

....

4 Eating junk food is bad. It can cause many health problems.

....

5 Going to the theatre is always worth it. It costs a lot of money.

....

6 It's a good idea to save money. It can be put in the bank.

....

7 Books will never lose their value. You can keep them forever.

....

8 Going to galleries is educational. It can sometimes be boring.

....

2 Match the parts and write sentences adding a relative clause. Use *who* or *which*.

Example:

The artist, who forged a painting, went to prison for ten years.

1	The artist	She is called Mary.	He became a famous actor.
2	The book	He was born in London.	It was full on Friday evening.
3	The theatre	The students performed.	She is going to study art.
4	Charlie Chaplin	He has borrowed it.	It was written by Oscar Wilde.
5	His sister	It was built in 1961.	He went to prison for ten years.
6	The play	He forged a painting.	It was published this year.

3 Rewrite each sentence so that it contains the information in brackets. Remember that no commas are necessary in defining relative clauses.

Example:

Mary cleaned the statues in the garden yesterday. (She lives next door.)

Mary, who lives next door, cleaned the statues in the garden yesterday.

1 She married a man. (She met him travelling on a cultural cruise.)

....

2 My house looks different from the others in the area. (It is black and white.)

....

3 I'm not very impressed by the painting of the woman. (She isn't really smiling.)

....

4 I want to buy the vintage dress. (I saw it yesterday in the shop window.)

....

5 Pass me the pen. (It is on the table.)

....

6 The woman stole the money. (She works in the university bookshop.)

....

7 I bought some new paint. (I now hate the colour as it's too dark.)

....

8 An old woman was injured yesterday in a car accident. (She was walking home from a concert.)

....

9 Hundreds of theatre-goers have been taken to hospital. (They were infected by the virus.)

....

10 The art exhibition attracts many overseas visitors. (It is held every summer.)

....

4 Correct the sentences below which contain errors.

1 That's the actress, who I told you about.

2 We went on a cultural holiday, that was just what I needed.

3 My sister, who is wearing the green dress, is playing the lead role.

4 Tomorrow which is my last day of the exhibition will be the best yet.

5 Artists who achieve world recognition are few and far between.

6 Fiction writers, often end up working on newspapers.

7 Impressionism, that is a style of painting, was considered controversial in its time.

8 Movie directors often choose classical music, which most people recognize when they hear it.

Reading

IELTS Reading Passage

You should spend about 20 minutes on **Questions 1–13**, which are based on the reading passage below.

Beauty of the beasts

By David Attenborough

Animals were the first things that human beings drew. Not plants. Not landscapes. Not even themselves. But animals. Why? The earliest known drawings are some 30,000 years old. They survive in the depths of caves in western Europe. The fact that some people crawled for half a mile or more along underground passages through the blackness is evidence enough that the production of such pictures was an act of great importance to these artists.

But what was their purpose? Maybe drawing was an essential part of the ceremonials they believed were necessary to ensure success in hunting. Maybe the paintings were intended not to bring about the death of the creatures portrayed but, on the contrary, to ensure their continued fertility so that the people would have a permanent source of meat. We cannot tell. One thing, however, is certain. These drawings are amazingly assured, wonderfully accurate and often breathtakingly beautiful.

This practice of painting images of animals on walls has persisted throughout our history. Five thousand years ago, when men in Egypt first began to build cities, they too inscribed images of animals on their walls.

There is no doubt about the function of at least some of these: the Egyptians worshipped animals as gods. But Egyptian artists also delighted in their natural beauty, for they adorned the walls of their own underground tombs with pictures. The mummified dead in the next world would surely wish to be reminded of the beauties and delights of this one.

By the 15th century however, the new scientific spirit of the Renaissance swept through Europe. Scholars began to examine the world with fresh eyes and to question the myths of the medieval mind. Leonardo da Vinci started to look at animals and plants in a new way. He wished to understand how they grew, moved and reproduced themselves, so he not only drew them in action but dissected their bodies.

Other scholars began to assess the variety of animal life that lay beyond their own countryside. For explorers travelling south down the coast of Africa, east to the Indies and west to the New World were bringing back completely new kinds of creatures.

Accordingly, the first in a series of illustrated books on the natural history of North America that culminated in 1827 in perhaps the greatest and certainly the most gigantic of all bird books, was entitled *The Birds of America*, by John James Audubon. Audubon hunted birds with an unquenchable passion and he drew them with equal enthusiasm. He thought that the standard static profiles, which, since ancient Egyptian times, had been the almost universal way of representing birds, gave no idea of their vivacity and grace. Audubon brought these dramatic drawings to Britain in order to get them engraved for reproduction. They were, however, among the last important natural history drawings to be printed in this way.

That was because a German printer had discovered that a line drawn with a wax pencil on a fine-grained limestone could be inked and printed. He refined the process to such an extent that soon the lithographic process was in use all over Europe, offering prints that could reproduce the most delicate lines directly from the artist's hand. The process led to a new flowering of natural history books.

Among the most spectacular were those produced by John Gould, who employed a series of artists, perhaps the most talented of whom was the 18-year-old Edward Lear, later to become more famous for his nonsense verse. Gould's sumptuous folio volumes appeared in imposing ranks on the shelves of aristocratic libraries throughout Britain.

By the beginning of the 20th century, it seemed that the age of great scientific natural history painting was coming to an end. Photography was beginning its reign, and it was soon possible to capture an exact image of the creature in front of you with the press of a finger.

Now the tiny electronic camera can record high-quality pictures in light so low that even the human eye has difficulty in perceiving what is in front of it. Optical cables can carry images from underground nest chambers at the end of long narrow tunnels. New vibration-proof mountings allow the camera to record close-ups of an animal while hovering in a helicopter a thousand feet above it.

You might think that these latest developments would finally bring to an end a tradition that stretches back 30,000 years. Not so. Today large-scale monographs devoted to particular groups of plants and animals are still produced by artists who welcome the double demands of aesthetic delight and scientific accuracy.

And they always will do. For no matter what the ostensible motive for their work, whether it is to lighten the reverential atmosphere of a monastery or to invoke animal spirits in a fertility ritual, to explore anatomy or to catalogue a discovery, there is a common denominator that links all these artists. It is the profound joy felt by all who observe the natural world with a sustained and devoted intensity.

Questions 1–9

Complete the summary using the list of words, **A–Q**, below.

Reasons for the human fascination with animals

Why early humans sketched animals and not other **1** .... from the world around them is a question that may never be answered. The **2** .... paintings drawn by man are located in underground formations, though we can only guess as to why they chose places that were so far underground. It has been suggested that they were part of a hunting **3** .... Other suggestions included that they were used encourage **4** .... in the animals so that people would not go hungry. However, all agree that the paintings themselves are both **5** .... and exquisite. Humans have **6** .... to use this 'walled' art form in many different ways throughout the ages. When the Egyptians were **7** .... their first settlements, they also drew animals on the walls. This was partly because they believed the animals were gods and **8** .... them as such. However, it was also because painters considered their attractiveness to be unadulterated, which is why they chose to paint them on the inside of their places of **9** ....

A background	**B** ritual	**C** fertile
D burial	**E** persist	**F** first
G build	**H** fertility	**I** continued
J nature	**K** scenes	**L** honoured
M essentials	**N** constructing	**O** simple
P precise	**Q** rich	

Questions 10–13

Look at the following list of statements about the drawing of animals (Questions 10–13) and the list of periods below.

Match each statement with the correct period, **A–C**.

NB You may use any letter more than once.

10 drew and then engraved the sketches for printing ....

11 a combination of old and new techniques employed ....

12 the rapid adoption of new line drawing technique ....

13 the early influence of anatomy on drawing ....

List of periods

A 14th–17th centuries

B 18th and 19th centuries

C 20th and 21st centuries

Think about the vocabulary in the reading passage. Scan the text again and find words/ collocations in the text that mean the same as a–z below.

a views of the countryside

....

b to move around on all fours

....

c shown in pictures

....

d to carve images onto something

....

e to decorate something

....

f chambers for dead bodies

....

g a period in time of great interest in the arts

....

h ancient stories, often untrue

....

i to cut open something, to analyze its structure

....

j highly-educated people

....

k very big

....

l a desire that cannot be fulfilled

....

m not moving

....

n energy/life

....

o to improve something

....

p printed

....

q poetry

....

r to catch (a moment in time)

....

s places where animals breed

....

t the real reason

....

u respectable

....

v something that is shared

....

w deep, true happiness

....

x continuous, uninterrupted

....

y loving and loyal to something

....

z a powerful force/passion

....

Writing

1 Read the question below and <u>underline</u> the key words and phrases.

(IELTS Writing Task 2)

WRITING TASK 2

You should spend about 40 minutes on this task.

Write about the following topic:

> *Children should not be encouraged to learn about the arts. Time in school should be purely devoted to academic subjects like language and maths.*
>
> *To what extent do you agree or disagree?*

Give reasons for your answer and include any relevant examples from your own knowledge or experience.

Write at least 250 words.

---

2 Answer questions **1–6** below giving examples from your own experience. Remember to keep your answers abstract.

1 Do you think most people are interested in the arts? Why/Why not?

2 Do children and young people study art, music and other art forms at school? Why/Why not?

3 Do you think people generally appreciate what they learned at school or do you think they should have learnt only scientific subjects? Why/Why not?

4 Imagine a world without music or art. Would the world be a better place if people <u>only</u> worked and never stopped to enjoy objects of beauty?

5 Is school the only place that children can learn about the arts?

6 What is the danger if the arts are not taught in school? Will all children be sure to learn about them?

3 Read the introductions (A & B) below. Decide which is better by answering the questions in the table by either adding a tick (✓) for yes and a cross (✗) for no.

> A Studying art and music is a waste of time. They are not important for children or adults and education should be devoted to learning about practical subjects that will help children get a job in the future. I always hated art and music and think they should be removed from the curriculum.

> B Studying art and music, while not essential, is vital so that children have a well-rounded education. Although they will not necessarily lead to children finding employment in these industries, a world without them would certainly be a quiet, colourless and sad place to live.

Area	Question	Introduction A	Introduction B
1 task response	1 Has the candidate addressed the question?		
2 coherence & cohesion	2 Are the sentences well-connected?		
3 grammar	3 Is the writer's opinion clear?		
4 vocabulary	4 Has the writer used a variety of structures?		
	5 Is the vocabulary: a interesting? b formal enough?		

4 Add your own ideas – supported by reasons – to the notes that have been started below. Use the ideas in the questions in exercise 2 to help you.

Arguments against teaching the arts at school:
1st idea:
children need to learn skills that will help them find a job in the future
reason: the world is much more competitive than before
2nd idea:
reason:

Arguments in favour of teaching the arts at school:
1st idea:
children need a break from studying books etc
reason: it opens their minds to different ways of thinking/seeing/feeling
2nd idea:
reason:

5 Use the notes to write your answer to the question, stating your opinion in the introduction as in exercise 3 above. Use supporting arguments.

1st paragraph: Introduction – state your opinion clearly

2nd paragraph: Opposing arguments to your opinion

3rd paragraph: Arguments supporting your opinion

4th paragraph: Summarize/re-iterate your opinion

11 Psychology and sociology

Vocabulary 1

Wordlist on page 217 of the coursebook.

The family

1 Change one word in each sentence below to make it correct.

   1 A grandmother is someone who is a daughter of one of your parents.

   2 An orphan is a woman who does not have parents.

   3 A niece is a son of someone's brother or sister.

   4 A household is all the children who live together in one dwelling.

   5 A widow is a man whose wife has died.

   6 A family list is a chart showing the past and present members of a family.

   7 A descendent is a relative who lived in the past.

   8 A sibling is someone who is either your brother or father.

2 Use one of the words above to replace the synonyms in *italics*. You may need to transform the word to refer to either the male, female or plural noun.

   1 'Past generations grew up in much larger *family units* than we do nowadays.'
   ....

   2 'The most famous *child without parents* was Oliver Twist from Charles Dickens' book based around the time of the French Revolution in the 18th century.' ....

   3 'I love my uncle. He says that I look like him when he was younger so I'm his favourite *son of all his siblings*.' ....

   4 'I never knew my *granny* very well as I grew up in a different country.' ....

   5 'I love my *brother and sister* even if we argue a lot sometimes.' ....

   6 'I'm proud that my *ancestral chart* spans many countries and cultures.' ....

   7 'My great aunt never remarried after her husband passed away. She was content to be a *woman whose husband has passed away*.' ....

   8 'I would love to be able to know more about my *relations who lived before I was born*.'
   ....

Word building

Suffixes *-hood* and *-ship*

1 Decide which of the following nouns take the suffix *-ship* or *-hood*. Write the complete word under the correct column.

brother	child	adult	member	neighbour	fellow
mother	partner	owner	champion		

-SHIP

1 ....
2 ....
3 ....
4 ....
5 ....

-HOOD

1 ....
2 ....
3 ....
4 ....
5 ....

2 Match the book title to its content:

TITLE	CONTENT
1 *A Brotherhood of Man*	a The story of a city neighbourhood
2 *A Snapshot of your Childhood*	b What membership to the oldest 'club' means
3 *The First Secret Society*	c How to survive the crying & sleepless nights
4 *How to Avoid Adulthood*	d An ideology of a world based on peace
5 *Urban Living: Together*	e The best and worst of the world championships
6 *Buying Your Own Home*	f An insight to memories we have all forgotten
7 *Motherhood: The Basics*	g An ownership guide to your first property
8 *World Cup Moments*	h The secret to staying young – on the inside

Reading

IELTS Reading Passage You should spend about 20 minutes on **Questions 1–13**, which are based on the reading passage below.

Psychology and the art of persuasion

Do you prefer cake to oranges? Do you sometimes buy something even if you don't need it? If the answer is yes, then you are a normal human doing what comes naturally, even if this is not necessarily what is good for you.

A Getting people to do what is good for them is notoriously difficult – just ask anyone who works in public health. Health officials spend their lives trying to persuade people to give up smoking, take more exercise and eat healthier food. In developing countries, persuading people to change their behaviour is key to reducing the ravages of AIDS, malaria, diarrhoea and other infectious diseases.

Their efforts are often in vain. A review of community anti-smoking interventions worldwide by researchers at the University of Vermont concluded that they had had virtually no effect. And a review by researchers at McMaster University in Hamilton, Ontario, Canada, of programmes designed to reduce unintended pregnancies among adolescents found that they, too, had been completely ineffective. Clearly, we need a new approach.

B Health promotion leans heavily on insights from late 20th-century cognitive psychology and the belief that our behaviour is driven by rational calculation. What it has yet to exploit is the revolution in brain science and psychology that has taken place over the past decade - and it is time it did. Neuroscience and evolutionary psychology can help us greatly in understanding and modifying human behaviour. They demonstrate that our decision-making is driven predominantly not by rationality but by emotions, which are seated in our ancient animal brain.

C The way we make decisions is driven more by emotions than rationality. Take the washing of hands with soap after using the toilet, one of the most widely disseminated health messages. More than a million lives could be saved each year if people washed their hands at key times,

because diarrhoeal and respiratory pathogens – the biggest child killers in the world today – are carried on people's hands. Despite this, our studies in developing countries suggest that fewer than 10 per cent of mothers do this, and mothers in developed countries are often not much better. Evidently, teaching people about germs is not enough.

D What our studies in Africa, Asia and Europe have shown is that people are much more likely to wash their hands if they are motivated to do so at a deeper emotional level – by disgust, or by the desire to conform to social norms and be respected by others, or to nurture and care for their offspring. In Ghana we found that people were failing to wash their hands because they did not perceive any contaminating matter on them: they did not see the yucky stuff, so they did not feel disgusted. So our job was to make people feel disgust, and we did this through a national campaign that included a television advertisement depicting a caring mother inadvertently contaminating her child's food via her hands after using the toilet. After watching it, 58 per cent of the mothers we asked said they had changed their hand-washing habits.

E There are many ways in which advances in brain science and psychology can help us change people's behaviour. Firstly, it is important to recognise that the brain works by associating experience with reward or punishment. People become addicted to smoking because their brain comes to associate it with pleasure. The way to break this is to use strong emotional triggers. Hence the recent 'give up before you clog up' anti-smoking campaign in the UK, which depicted a cigarette oozing fat. Likewise, if you want to get people to take up healthy habits, you have to associate them with strong rewards. So while the promise that running will make you healthy might not be enough to persuade people to take it up, the suggestion that it will make you more attractive as a mate could do the trick.

F Secondly, evolution has programmed us to be lazy, to conserve energy where possible, so healthy choices have to be easy ones. Junk food is attractive because it resembles food that was rare and desirable in the environment in which we evolved: energy-dense, sweet and fatty. Nowadays it is available everywhere, and cheaply. Food policy should concentrate on making healthy foods equally easy to get hold of.

G Thirdly, surprise is crucial. Emotions only kick in to interrupt a habit when the brain detects that an impending reward is noticeably greater or less than what it has learned to expect – think how you would feel on finding a cockroach in a bowl of delicious soup. Health campaigns have to continually reinvent themselves and grab people's attention.

Changing behaviour means understanding our deepest desires. To break unhealthy habits, campaigners need to target the emotions, because they are the decision-makers. Where the heart leads, the habits will follow.

Questions 1–7

The reading passage has seven sections, **A–G**.

Which section contains the following information?

1 a potential number of deaths that could be avoided

2 how encouragement is used to change habits that affect both lifestyle and disease

3 what ultimately causes people to alter bad behaviour

4 why making positive and negative connections have an effect

5 the theories that were relied considerably on to create campaigns

6 an example of a cleanliness campaign that worked

7 the appeal of fast food, even though it is unhealthy

Questions 8–11

Complete the sentences below.

Choose **NO MORE THAN TWO WORDS** from the passage for each answer.

8 Health campaigns around the world have consistently had almost .... in making people give up smoking.

9 After using more up-to-date methods in studies, researchers found that women involved in a Ghanaian campaign modified their ....

10 The use of strong .... is suggested as the way to break the correlation between smoking and pleasure in the brain.

11 If the goal is to make people choose healthy food over junk food, then decision makers need to make the latter .... to come by.

Questions 12 and 13

Choose **TWO** letters, **A–E**.

Which **TWO** possible reasons why humans change their habits are mentioned by the writer of the passage?

A respect from others

B rational emotions

C cognitive psychology

D shocking truths

E making calculations

1 When approaching a text, there are two main ways in which you can focus on new language: You can check the meaning of individual words or analyze a whole group ('chunk') of words and try to get the meaning from the context. Which do you find helps you more?

2 Read the 'chunks' from the article and cross out the alternative that is not correct.

1 'Health promotion leans heavily on insights from late 20th-century cognitive psychology ...'

Health promotion *only uses/largely uses* 20th century cognitive psychology.

2 ' ... our behaviour is driven by rational calculation.'

... *logical decisions/illogical decisions* push us to behave in certain ways.'

3 ' ... emotions, which are seated in our ancient animal brain.'

... emotions *sit/come from* a part of the brain that *relates to/is unrelated to* our animal past.

4 ' ... the desire to conform to social norms ... '

... a wish *to be like others/to be different from others ...* '

5 ' ... they did not perceive any contaminating matter on them.'

... they *could see/could not see* anything *infectious/clean* on them ...

6 ' ... a caring mother inadvertently contaminating her child's food ... '

... a mother made her child's food *dirty/healthy on purpose/accidentally* ...

7 ' ... the brain works by associating experience with reward or punishment.'

... the brain *doesn't work if there is no reward/makes connections with the end result.*

8 ' ... depicted a cigarette oozing fat.'

... showed a cigarette *with fat coming out/making you fat.*

9 ' ... the suggestion that it will make you more attractive as a mate could do the trick.'

... suggesting that something will make you more attractive could *work/be difficult.*'

10 'Where the heart leads, the habits will follow.'

If you want people to change their behaviour, you should try to *change their habits/affect their emotions.*'

Listening

👁 2.3 **SECTION 1** Questions 1–10

Questions 1–5

Complete the form below.

Write **NO MORE THAN THREE WORDS AND/OR A NUMBER** for each answer.

Sociology research project survey	
Example	*Answer*
Survey on:	community centres
Age:	1 ....
Postcode:	2 ....
COMPUTER FACILITIES	
ALREADY USED	
Where?	3 ....
SPORTS FACILITIES	
ALREADY USED	
Where?	4 ....
EDUCATION FACILITIES	
ALREADY USED	
Where?	5 ....

Questions 6–10

IMPROVEMENTS FOR THE COMMUNITY CENTRE	
New sports:	6 .... and ....
Classes organized only for:	7 ....
Education classes:	8 .... and ....
Willing to pay about:	9 £ .... for new classes
Possible frequency of visits, if improvements made?	10 .... a week

> **Language focus**

 Grammar reference on page 224 of the coursebook.

Conditionals 2

1 Read the examples of conditional structures below and <u>underline</u> the verbs in both clauses.

1 If I <u>give up</u> caffeine, I'<u>ll sleep</u> better. 1ˢᵗ d

2 If I gave up eating junk food, I would live for longer. ....

3 If I hadn't started smoking, I would have saved a lot of money. ....

4 If I hadn't started smoking, I would be healthier now. ....

5 If I understood more about how the mind works, it would make it easier to give up smoking. ....

2 Identify the type of conditional and then match the sentences 1–5 in exercise 1 to their meaning a–d below. One type of conditional is used twice.

a relates to a situation in the past with a past result

b relates to a situation in the past with a present result

c relates to a hypothetical situation with a result now or in the future

d relates to a real situation with a result now or in the future

3 Rewrite sentence 1 from exercise 2 using the word in brackets.

i Unless I give up... [unless]

ii .... [provided that]

iii .... [should]

iv .... [supposing]

4 Complete the sentences below, identifying the type of conditional in brackets.

1 Unless we learn about our family tree, ... [.........]

2 The world would be a fairer place if .... [.........]

3 Should people around the world mix more .... [.........]

4 If football fans hadn't been so unsociable after the match .... [.........]

5 Supposing emotional intelligence were taught at school .... [.........]

6 If we know that eating junk food is bad, why.............................? [.........]

7 Unless we live to be 200 years old, ... [.........]

8 If humans had not been born with a spirit of adventure, ... [.........]

Writing

1 Look at the Task 2 question and the students' notes 1–7 below and decide whether they agree or disagree with the opinion.

WRITING TASK 2

You should spend about 40 minutes on this task.

Write about the following topic:

> *Although societies around the world are richer and more advanced than ever before, people are not as happy as they used to be. Some people, therefore, feel that in order to be happy it is better for people to be poor and less advanced.*
>
> *Do you agree or disagree with this opinion?*

Write at least 250 words.

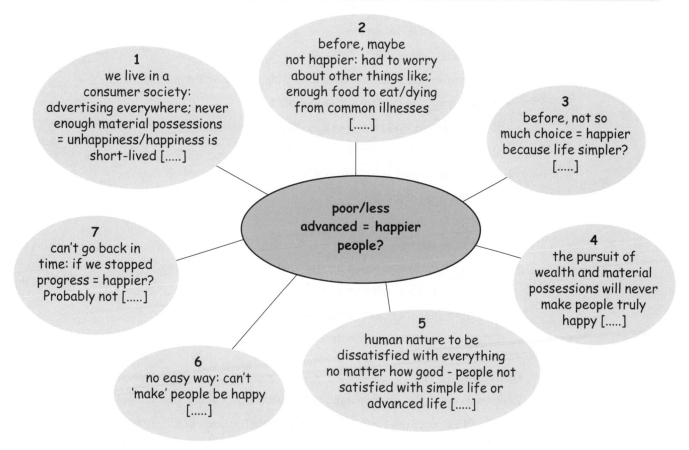

2 Use the notes to write your own answer to the question. Remember to check your answer for errors. Compare your answer with the model answer in the key.

Listening

⊙ 2.4 **SECTION 2** Questions 11–20

Questions 11–15

Choose the correct letter, **A**, **B** or **C**.

11 The park which makes up Hampstead Heath is

   A very large.

   B fairly large.

   C fairly small.

12 According the speaker, Hampstead underground station is

   A the shallowest in the system.

   B the deepest in the system.

   C the oldest in London.

13 The speaker suggests that after their walk people might want to

   A have a meal in the famous restaurants.

   B avoid Hampstead village as it is very busy.

   C visit Hampstead village to look at the shops.

14 The houses in the Vale of the Heath are built

   A on the edge of the heath.

   B on the heath itself.

   C opposite the heath.

15 The speaker advises walkers to remove their headphones to

   A hear the silence away from the traffic.

   B ensure they are not being followed.

   C listen to the noises in the park.

Questions 16–20

Which activity can be done at each of the following locations on the heath?

Choose **FIVE** answers from the box and write the correct letter, **A–G**, next to questions 16–20.

Activities

   A have picnics

   B go fishing

   C view London

   D have a swim

   E attend concerts

   F watch plays

   G have snacks

Locations on the Heath

16 Kenwood House ....

17 grassy slopes ....

18 open-air stage ....

19 ponds ....

20 Parliament Hill ....

Vocabulary 1

Wordlist on page 217 of the Coursebook.

Adjectives with multiple meanings

1 <u>Underline</u> the correct meaning in brackets of the words in *italics* in the sentences below.

  1 He was *curious* when he travelled abroad, so he picked up lots of ideas and information. (unusual/very interested in learning new things)

  2 She was very *different* from everyone else, but that's what made her very appealing. (various/not the same)

  3 The memories of my visit to Japan are *fresh* in my mind. (not old/new and different)

  4 I must have looked like an *alien*, because when I first appeared my clothes were very different and I was so tall. (being from another planet/new and different)

  5 Travelling by high-speed train over long distances is not *novel*, but it is still exciting for most people. (a fictional book/new and original)

  6 Some of the customs were *foreign* to me, but I soon adapted to the way of life. (unfamiliar/from overseas)

  7 The vehicle was completely *new*; it had never even been on the road before. (different from the one before/not used yet)

  8 The behaviour of the animals was *strange* as they usually behaved normally with visitors. (out of the ordinary/ not familiar)

IELTS Reading Passage

You should spend about 20 minutes on **Questions 1–13**, which are based on the reading passage below.

The Scenic Route into Switzerland

Travelling by train in Europe is one of life's great pleasures, where the journey is as important as the destination.

Few countries lend themselves to sightseeing by train as well as Switzerland. In this country of mountains, lakes and valleys, it's the ideal way to travel. Avoiding airport hassles, travelling there by rail adds an extra dimension to the holiday. There's great pleasure in watching Europe's landscapes unfold through picture windows.

The sense of Continental style begins as soon as you leave London's St Pancras International station aboard a sleek Eurostar train. It is pleasantly relaxing to watch the Kent countryside zip by. At Brussels Midi station it's an easy connection to a German intercity ICE train, speeding along to Cologne in comfort levels above even those of Eurostar and the TGV.

The entire journey from London, through France, Belgium and Germany, takes around six hours, leaving plenty of energy for a walk through the centre of Cologne and a visit to the spectacular cathedral there. The city has plenty of good hotels and restaurants and is ideal for an overnight stay.

Then from Cologne to Chur, Germany to Switzerland, via towns with evocative names – Koblenz, Mainz, Mannheim and Baden Baden – and the cities of Basel and Zurich. It's a grand day's travelling.

Through the domed observation car of a EuroCity train you see castles standing sentry over the wide and winding River Rhine, where laden barges travel low in the choppy green water. Neat houses clamber into tree-covered hillsides punctuated by churches with needle spires and baroque bonnets topping sturdy towers. There are tall cliffs and vineyard-terraced slopes, jagged rocks and sandy islands green with trees; red-roofed towns and farming villages, orchards and industry, the spectacular Rhine Gorge and Zurich's vast lake.

Chur was under Roman rule for 400 years, when the region was known as Rhaetia, and for centuries has been a transport hub to the north of the passes over the Alps. The first train steamed towards the town in 1858. Today the Arosa Railway travels through the city's centre before it begins its winding climb up to the famed mountain resort of Arosa. And Chur, Switzerland's oldest city, is the starting point for the narrow-gauge Rhaetian Railway's Bernina Express to Tirano in Italy, the picture windows of its domed observation cars cleaned to a sparkle.

There are 'walls' of tall pines and dark forests, steep drops, forbidding bare rock face, curtain waterfalls and glimpses of turquoise water far below. To breach this seemingly impassable landscape, engineers faced steep mountain slopes and tumbling rocks to construct three bridges and 14 tunnels. The train bursts into light for mere seconds before plunging once more into darkness.

On what has been called the most ingenious railway line ever built, the Bernina Express travels on a 'spiral staircase', twisting upwards through five loop tunnels, two normal tunnels, crossing nine viaducts and going under two galleries before reaching Preda, which sits nearly 6000ft above sea level.

The journey continues through the Albula tunnel, Europe's highest subterranean alpine crossing, into Switzerland's Romansch-speaking Engadine region. Emerging from the tunnel, you may well find that the weather has changed. And, being at a watershed, the rivers are flowing in the opposite direction!

The Bernina Pass, 'land of eternal ice', is a watershed – the rivers flow to the Po and into the Adriatic – and a linguistic boundary. South of the Pass, Italian dialects are spoken. At 7381ft (around 2250m) the station of Ospizio Bernina is the highest point on the journey.

Glaciers separate mountains and from Alp Grumm there's a panoramic view of snowfields and a countless array of mountain peaks. Although Lake Poschiavo lies way below, it is hard to believe that in an hour's time the train will be in Italy, in a Mediterranean climate among palm trees and flowering oleanders.

From sunshine and geraniums, through layers of snow covered mountains, by glacier tongues and long-drop waterfalls, to green-swathed valleys and a taste of Italy all in three and a half hours – the Bernina Express journey is quite an experience. And a very comfortable one.

If the changing scenery is extreme and memorable, so too is the way the train deals with immense gradients, and with not a cogwheel or rack rail in sight. On the Bernina line the train climbs 228ft (70m) of height in every 3280ft (1000m) of distance covered. And down again.

Questions 1–3

Do the following statements agree with the information given in the reading passage?
Write:

YES if the statement agrees with the views of the writer

NO if the statement contradicts the views of the writer

NOT GIVEN if it is impossible to say what the writer thinks about this

1 Looking at the sights in Switzerland by train is a boring experience.

2 As soon as the train leaves from London, it feels like being in another country.

3 The towns mentioned in Germany have unusual names.

Questions 4–6

Answer the questions below.

Choose **NO MORE THAN TWO WORDS** from the passage for each answer.

4 Where does the train that terminates in Tirano, Italy start from?

5 Which alpine crossing in the Engadine region is the highest in Europe?

6 What can you see many of from Alp Grumm?

Questions 7–13

Complete the summary below.

Choose **NO MORE THAN TWO WORDS AND/OR A NUMBER** from the passage for each answer.

The Bernina Express

The Bernina Express is considered the **7** .... railway that has ever been constructed due to the complexity of the landscape through which it travels. The mountainous region must have seemed **8** .... with the **9** .... encountering many difficulties in construction. The railway on which the Express runs twists like a **10** .... as it goes up through a range of man-made constrictions to reach a height of **11** .... feet above sea level. The Bernina Pass marks the **12** .... between two rivers as well as a **13** ....

1 There is a lot of descriptive language in the article. Write the words and phrases used in the passage to describe the following in the table:

○	**1** train travel	'one of life's great pleasures'
○	**2** Cologne	
○	**3** River Rhine	
○	**4** houses	
○	**5** hills, slopes & mountains	
○	**6** churches	
○	**7** towns & villages	
○	**8** trees	
○	**9** Italy	

2 Use a dictionary to check any words you do not know.

Word building

Words related to memory

1 Decide which word formed from the root 'mem-' is being described below. Write your answer in the space provided.

   1 If you lose this, you won't be able to find your way home from abroad.

   ....

   2 When people retire, they often write these in their spare time. ....

   3 IELTS candidates shouldn't try to do this in the speaking test. It will interrupt their fluency.

   ....

   4 Tourists sometimes visit these monuments to pay their respects to the dead.

   ....

   5 People collect these in the hope they will be worth money one day. ....

   6 People leave these on your desk/email when they haven't got time to write a long message. ....

   7 If you remember a holiday after many years, it's because it was ....

   8 It's polite to do this to new people's names as soon as possible. ....

   9 People often keep these to remind them of a place/person/time, even if it's not worth anything in monetary terms. ....

   10 If you do lots of interesting things with your life when you are young, you should have lots of these to make yourself smile when you are old. ....

2 Write the words from exercise 1 in the correct column below.

ADJECTIVE	VERB	NOUN
....	....	....
	....	....
		....
		....
		....
		....

> **Language focus**

 Grammar reference on page 225 of the coursebook.

Articles

1 The grammatical names of articles can help you understand why they are used. Look at the three types of article on the left and match them with the examples on the right.

Type	Example
1 indefinite article	**i** I went to a party.
2 definite article	**ii** I like parties.
3 zero article	**iii** The party on Saturday was great.

2 Read some of these more detailed 'rules' and decide whether they go with the indefinite, definite or zero article. The first is done for you.

1 Used the first time you mention a non-specific noun. *indefinite – a/an.*

2 Used the second time you mention a noun; now specific. ....

3 Used to talk in general about nouns. (Plural when countable.) ....

4 Used to refer to specific things. ....

5 Used to refer to any one, of many. ....

6 Used with singular, countable nouns. ....

7 Used with countries made up of states, kingdoms, republics, emirates. ....

3 Choose the correct option using the guidelines in each case and match it to the rules 1–7 in exercise 2.

1 You want to refer to a singular noun, for the first time.

'There is *a/an/the/–* map in my bag. Can you pass it to me, please?' Rule: ....

2 There are guidebooks on the table. You want the blue one. You say:

'Pass me *a/an/the/–* blue guidebook, please.' Rule: ....

3 You need new bandages. You ask your friend to buy you some. You say:

'Can you buy *a/an/the/–* bandages when you're out, please?' Rule: ....

4 You buy one new bicycle. You tell your friend about your new purchase.

'I bought *a/an/the/–* new bicycle at the weekend.' Rule: ....

5 You ask the same friend if they want to have a look at it.

'Would you like to have a look at *a/an/the/–* bike?' Rule: ....

6 You want to travel to the Middle East this winter. You say:

'I'm thinking about going to *a/an/the/–* United Arab Emirates.' Rule: ....

7 You need to buy a compass. You ask your friend to lend you one as he has several. You say:

'Could I borrow *a/an/the/–* compass, please.' Rule: ....

IELTS Writing Task 2 4 Find and correct the errors relating to articles in the text below.

'Gap Years' originated in the UK in the 1960s when young Brits headed off to the infamous 'hippie trail' in India. But an idea truly took off in the 1990s.

'Gap Years' are a common experience in a United Kingdom, and across the Europe. In the United States, however, not many people are familiar with the idea. A gap year is a time taken off between two stages of life—usually by the students between high school and college—to travel, volunteer and explore a world.

But Gap Years can also be taken by the adults before moving onto the new profession, a new marriage or simply as career break. Gap Years are meant not to just explore new places and cultures, but also to learn the new skills and discover new things about yourself.

Writing

1 Read the Task 2 question below and then answer the questions.

WRITING TASK 2

You should spend about 40 minutes on this task.

Write about the following topic:

> *Some people believe that travelling alone is far better than travelling with a group. Others believe that this is dangerous and should not be encouraged by the parents of young people.*
>
> *Discuss both these views and give your own opinion.*

Give reasons for your answer and include any relevant examples from your own knowledge and experience.

Write at least 250 words.

---

1 Is it acceptable to only talk about one of these opinions?

2 How many paragraphs would you need to answer the question? Why?

3 Which body paragraph is it better to start off with: the one that's the same as your opinion or the one that's the opposite of your opinion? Why?

2 Match each idea a–e with 'alone' or 'group' view. If it is irrelevant mark it with an 'X'

IDEAS

a Going on holiday is good for one's health and everyone should do it at least once a year.

b If people are involved in any trouble, they can usually rely on help from the group.

c It is easier to be 'led astray' by strangers as they see lone visitors as an easy target.

d Travelling alone means that you don't have to follow the decisions of the group.

e Travelling alone allows people to meet more local people.

3 Match the relevant ideas from exercise 2 to their supporting arguments (i-iv).

i There is safety in numbers.

ii They can help people both with moral and financial support if they need it.

iii Therefore, people can have a richer experience of the country they are visiting.

iv People can do and see exactly what they like and not waste time.

4 Write your own response to the essay question above, using the ideas to help you.

⑬ The importance of infrastructure

Vocabulary

Wordlist on page 218 of the coursebook.

Nouns related to systems

1 Decide which aspect of infrastructure is being described in 1–8 below.

1 letters, emails, messages and phone calls are part of this system which is to do with contacting people. _ _ _ _ _ _ _ _ _ _ _ _ _ (13)

2 a factory where oil is cleaned for commercial use _ _ _ _ _ _ _ _ (8)

3 the process of moving people or things from one place to another, usually in a vehicle _ _ _ _ _ _ _ _ _ (9)

4 an object sent into space to travel around the earth in order to receive and send information _ _ _ _ _ _ _ _ _ (9)

5 a form of energy that can produce light, heat and power for machines, computers, televisions, etc. _ _ _ _ _ _ _ _ _ _ _ (11)

6 in computing, 'www' stands for world wide _ _ _ (3)

2 Match the sentence halves **1–8** with **a–h** to form news bulletins.

1 The transport system ground to a halt this morning due to the adverse

2 The scarcity of oil has caused prices to reach an all-time-high as wells and

3 The threat of a virus which attacks a network's fibre optics, potentially bringing down the world's communications

4 The Global Positioning Satellite system (GPS) was again in trouble last night after it sent another lorry into a low-rise

5 The future of gas as a sustainable fuel source looks uncertain as further

6 Water purification plants are now in common use in countries which suffer problems with fresh water supplies as they allow previously undrinkable

7 The inventor of the worldwide web was honoured with a Nobel prize for engineering as his creation now provides us with access to

8 There was a huge power cut across most of the country as storms brought down

---

a salty water to be desalinated.

b systems was described as imminent.

c weather conditions which have affected all major routes.

d pylons and power lines.

e bridge after the receiver dish failed.

f problems with the new proposed pipeline continue.

g refineries struggle to cope with demand.

h information at our fingertips through a complex system of servers.

Word building

Modal verbs to adjectives

1 Write the adjectives in the box below next to the modal that corresponds to their meaning.

likely	possible	probable	certain	unnecessary	necessary
expected	obligatory	able	compulsory	optional	essential
permissible	unlikely				

    1 must   ....

    2 will   ....

    3 probably will   ....

    4 can/could   ....

    5 probably won't   ....

    6 do not have to   ....

    7 should   ....

2 Rewrite the sentences below using the adjectives in brackets. You will have to change the structure of the sentence.

Example:

We must do our best to lower carbon emissions. (essential)

It is essential that we do our best to lower carbon emissions.

    1 We need to invest in less polluting technologies. (necessary)

    ....

    2 Unless free public transport is maintained for older people, there will be more congestion. (certain to)

    ....

    3 As the cost of petrol rises, people will probably use bicycles more. (likely to)

    ....

    4 More people will probably migrate to cities in the next twenty years. (probable)

    ....

    5 With the new technologies available, major cities can now choose to introduce driverless trains. (possible)

    ....

    6 Taking a train to travel long distances probably won't be as popular as flying. (unlikely that)

    ....

    7 People do not have to know how computer systems work, but it helps when looking for employment in many infrastructure industries. (unnecessary for)

    ....

    8 Airlines are expected to introduce more fuel-efficient planes in the near future. (should)

    ....

IELTS Reading Passage   You should spend about 20 minutes on **Questions 1–13**, which are based on the reading passage below.

Building BRICs* of growth

Record spending on infrastructure will help to sustain rapid growth in emerging economies

A THE biggest investment boom in history is underway. Over half of the world's infrastructure investment is now taking place in emerging economies, where sales of excavators have risen more than fivefold since 2000. In total, emerging economies are likely to spend an estimated $1.2 trillion[1] on roads, railways, electricity, telecommunications and other projects this year, equivalent to 6% of their combined GDPs – twice the average infrastructure-investment ratio in developed economies. Largely as a result, total fixed investment in emerging economies could increase by a staggering 16% in real terms this year, according to HSBC, whereas in rich economies it is forecast to be flat. Such investment will help support economic growth this year as America's economy stalls – and for many years to come.

B Compounding this year's figure, Morgan Stanley predicts that emerging economies will spend $22 trillion (in today's prices) on infrastructure over the next ten years, of which China will account for 43%. China is already spending around 12% of its GDP on infrastructure. Indeed, China has spent more (in real terms) in the past five years than in the whole of the 20th century. Last year Brazil launched a four-year plan to spend $300 billion to modernise its road network, power plants and ports. The Indian government's latest five-year plan has ambitiously pencilled in nearly $500 billion in infrastructure projects. Russia, the Gulf states and other oil exporters are all pouring part of their higher oil revenues into fixed investment.

C Good infrastructure has always played a leading role in economic development, from the roads and aqueducts of ancient Rome to Britain's railway boom in the mid-19th century. But

* BRICs = Brazil, Russia, India and China

never before has infrastructure spending been so large as a share of world GDP. This is partly because more countries are now industrialising than ever before, but also because China and others are investing at a much brisker pace than rich economies ever did. Even at the peak of Britain's railway mania in the 1840s, total infrastructure investment was only around 5% of GDP.

D   Infrastructure investment can yield big economic gains. Building roads or railways immediately boosts output and jobs, but it also helps to spur future growth – provided the money is spent wisely. Better transport helps farmers to get their produce to cities, and manufacturers to export their goods overseas. Countries with the lowest transport costs tend to be more open to foreign trade and so enjoy faster growth. Clean water and sanitation also raise the quality of human capital, thereby lifting labour productivity. The World Bank estimates that a 1% increase in a country's infrastructure stock is associated with a 1% increase in the level of GDP. Other studies have concluded that East Asia's much higher investment in infrastructure explains a large part of its faster growth than Latin America.

E   A recent report by Goldman Sachs argues that infrastructure spending is not just a cause of economic growth, but a consequence of it. As people get richer and more of them live in towns, the demand for electricity, transport, sanitation and housing increases. This mutually reinforcing relationship leads to higher investment and growth. The bank has developed a model that uses expected growth in income, urbanisation and population to forecast future infrastructure demands.

F   Urbanisation has the biggest impact on electricity requirements. Goldman calculates that a 1% increase in the share of people living in cities leads to a 1.8% increase in demand for installed capacity. A 1% rise in income per head leads to a 0.5% increase in demand. Putting this together, electricity capacity may have to surge by 140% in China and by 80% in India over the next decade. Air travel – and hence airports – will see the fastest growth in demand, because it is by far the most sensitive to income: a 1% increase in income per person leads to a 1.4% increase in the number of passengers travelling by air. The number of air passengers could jump by more than 350% in China and by 200% in India over the next decade.

G   China's faster growth in income per head and its more rapid pace of urbanisation mean that it is likely to pull even further ahead of India on most infrastructure measures. China could add 13 times as many fixed-line phones as India over the decade, seven times as many air passengers and six times as much electricity capacity. Brazil and Russia, which are already much more urbanised and relatively richer (implying slower growth in income), will also see more modest growth in infrastructure.

H   The infrastructure boom has global implications too. Increased investment means more imports of capital equipment, which will help to slim current-account surpluses in China and elsewhere, and so reduce global imbalances. Rising demand for building materials will keep commodity prices high.

I   Last, but not least, will be the negative impact on the environment. An expected 75% increase in emerging economies' electricity demand over the next decade will worsen air pollution and global warming. Many fear that China's Three Gorges Dam, the world's largest hydroelectric project, could cause environmental damage. China's national bird, the red-crowned crane, is an endangered species. Some people may wish that the 'construction crane' was also breeding less rapidly.

Glossary: 1 a trillion = the number 1,000,000,000,000

Questions 1–5

The reading passage has nine paragraphs, **A–I**.

Which paragraph contains the following information?

1   the quantity of digging machinery bought in comparison to the past

2   how spending money on infrastructure like transport systems leads to more work

3   a reference to two past examples of increases in construction

4   how personal wealth and increased travel are related

5   why more infrastructure is needed if people migrate to urban areas

Questions 6–9

Do the following statements agree with the views of the writer in the reading passage?

Write:

YES	if the statement agrees with the views of the writer
NO	if the statement contradicts the views of the writer
NOT GIVEN	if it is impossible to say what the writer thinks of this

6 An unprecedented growth in spending is taking place in emerging economies.

7 Increased spending on infrastructure is the best way to improve a country's economy.

8 The main reason spending is high is because so many countries are industrializing.

9 The construction boom will not have an effect in countries around the world.

Questions 10–13

Choose the correct letter, **A**, **B**, **C** or **D**.

10 In the current year, emerging economies may spend

    A their money on improving communication.

    B twice as much as developed countries did.

    C 16% more than developed countries on infrastructure.

    D 6% more on projects compared to last year.

11 Money can be made from

    A investing in the future.

    B being open to trade.

    C helping farmers move to cities.

    D constructing transport links.

12 The economies in East Asia are growing faster than

    A in Britain.

    B infrastructure stock.

    C in Latin America.

    D expected in this decade.

13 The environmental impact on infrastructure development will

    A include increased contamination of the air.

    B put pressure on the world's resources.

    C cause more species to be endangered.

    D lead to a 75 per cent increase in pollution.

Listening

👁 **2.5 SECTION 3 Questions 21–30**

Questions 21–25

How do the speakers describe the green urban planning options?

Choose **FIVE** descriptions from the box and write the correct letter, **A–G**, next to questions 21–25.

Descriptions	
A dangerous	
B too expensive	
C too many objections	
D disruptive	
E too simple	
F unpractical	
G unsuccessful	

21 green belt ....
22 decentralization ....
23 new towns ....
24 brownfield sites ....
25 pedestrianized zones ....

Questions 26–28

Choose the correct letter, **A**, **B** or **C**.

26 Which area is Jack having the most problems with?

    A Understanding the statistics.

    B The lack of material.

    C The selection of statistics.

27 What has been central to Curitiba's success?

    A Central government intervention.

    B Working together with residents.

    C Giving responsibility to strategists.

28 Why does the transport system work so well?

    A There are cheap fares for the poor and elderly.

    B Bicycles can use the bus lanes.

    C There is a low car ownership.

Questions 29 and 30

Choose **TWO** letters, **A–E**.

Which does the tutor suggest are the **TWO** areas Jack needs to focus on?

A the amount of parkland

B the employment strategy

C the pedestrianized zones

D the recycling scheme

E the suburban areas

Language focus

 Grammar reference on page 225 of the coursebook.

Concession

1 Choose a suitable synonym for the original word in italics.

1 *Although* constructing new roads is important for a country's economy, it should not be at the expense of the environment. (*but/while*)

2 *While* I agree investing in the future may be a good idea, it is also important to focus on the present. (*much as/might*)

3 There are more jobs available in cities, *though* they might not necessarily be better ones. (*but/while*)

4 *While* there are many reasons for people being wealthier than before, it is mainly down to improvements in education. (*but/though*)

5 None of the information in the article was new to me, but it was interesting *nonetheless*. (*much as/nevertheless*)

6 *Much as* I can understand your point of view, I would have to disagree with you. (*while/but*)

2 Practise conceding, but ultimately disagreeing with these extreme points of view. Use the words given in brackets.

Example:

The only way to improve your English is to memorize new words! (while/this/important,/not only way)

While memorizing is important, it is not the only way to improve your English.

1 Travelling abroad is a waste of money! (although/it/expensive/not waste)

2 Riding a bicycle is slow and boring! (it/may/slow/but/not boring)

3 Everyone finds speed limits annoying! They're completely unnecessary. (much as/feel/they/annoying/necessary/as/save lives)

4 The wheel was the most important invention ever. (though/it/useful,/not most important)

Writing

IELTS Task 1

1 Read the Task 1 question below and then put the information a–i into the correct order.

WRITING TASK 1

You should spend about 20 minutes on this task.

The chart below shows the number of international visits made from the United Kingdom.

Summarise the information by selecting and reporting the main features, and make comparisons where relevant.

Write at least 150 words.

International travel from the UK (millions)

	1981	1986	1991	1996	1998	1999	2000
Air	11.4	16.4	20.4	27.9	34.3	37.5	41.4
Sea	7.7	8.6	10.4	10.7	10.5	10.4	9.6
Channel Tunnel	.	.	.	3.5	6.1	5.9	5.8
All visits abroad	19	24.9	30.8	42.1	50.9	53.9	56.8

a In 1981, 19 million trips were made abroad from the UK, of which 11.4 million were made by air and 7.7 million by sea.

b Ten years later, the number of people travelling by air had almost doubled, whereas travelling by sea had only increased by approximately half its original total.

c The table shows the number of overseas visits made from the UK during the years 1981-2000. The data is organized into the types of transport used.

d It is clear that travelling abroad became increasingly popular over the period.

e Sea travel was still in second place but its popularity had suffered as more people opted for the Channel Tunnel. There were just under 1 million fewer visits by sea than its peak in 1996.

f In contrast, the Channel Tunnel reached its peak of popularity in 1998 when numbers almost doubled from 3.5 million when it opened to 6.1 million.

g For the first time in 1996, travel via the Channel Tunnel was possible but numbers were relatively small in comparison to the two other modes of transport.

h By the end of the millennium its popularity had also decreased though only slightly with 5.8 million visits made via the Tunnel.

i By 2000, however, air travel was by far the most popular option with 41.4 million visits a year.

2   Look at the table and write your own answer.

WRITING TASK 1

You should spend about 20 minutes on this task.

The table below shows the number of international visits into the United Kingdom.

Summarise the information by selecting and reporting the main features, and make comparisons where relevant.

Write at least 150 words.

Visits to the UK by overseas residents (millions)

	1981	1986	1991	1996	1998	1999	2000
Air	6.9	8.9	8.9	8.9	8.9	8.9	8.9
Sea	4.6	5	5	5	5	5	5
Channel Tunnel	.	.	.	.	.	.	.
All visits to the United Kingdom	11.5	13.9	13.9	13.9	13.9	13.9	13.9

14 Money and happiness

Vocabulary

Wordlist on page 218 of the coursebook.

Money matters

1   Match the words 1–10 below with their meanings a–j on the right. There may be more than one possible answer.

1 counterfeit money		a	the money a government has to spend
2 family finances		b	a person addicted to buying things
3 government money		c	money collected from people's taxes
4 paper money		d	after paying the bills, the money that's left over
5 public money/taxpayers' money		e	fake, illegal money
6 shopaholic		f	a person who can't control their money
7 spending money		g	the money which a family has to spend
8 spendthrift		h	money collected from a company for advertising its products
9 sponsorship money		i	an amount of money owed to a person or organization
10 debt		j	money in note, as opposed to coin, form

2   Decide whether the words in *italics* collocate with the verb in each case. In some cases all the words may be possible.

1   boost *finances/money/wealth*   ....

2   borrow *finances/money/wealth*   ....

3   build *finances/money/wealth*   ....

4   control *finances/money/wealth*   ....

5   deposit *finances/money/wealth*   ....

6   devalue *finances/money/wealth*   ....

7   have *finances/money/wealth*   ....

8   hoard *finances/money/wealth*   ....

9   inherit *finances/money/wealth*   ....

10 squander *finances/money/wealth*   ....

IELTS Section 4

Listening

⊙ **2.6 SECTION 4 Questions 31–40**

Questions 31–40

Complete the notes below.

Write **NO MORE THAN TWO WORDS** for each answer.

Economics course guidelines

During lectures

Students:

- will receive information about economics and the **31** .... to concentrate on

- will be provided with information about the subject

- will be provided with a framework for further study

- will have an opportunity to be taught by a **32** .... in the field

- will take part in the learning culture in **33** ....

Common problems students have with techniques used in lectures

- may not develop **34** .... : no immediate questions

- newer techniques help improve **35** .... more than lectures

How to avoid problems and make learning easier

- leave time to read **36** .... on the booklist

- test yourself with quizzes

- if you have had a **37** .... , revise what you previously learned

- use the web to do more **38** ....

- check the sources of information on the web are **39** ....

- **40** .... with your classmates

---

Word building

Values and beliefs

1 Use the definitions below to help you complete the grid with plural nouns from the coursebook. When you have finished you will find the solution to 1 down refers to a person who believes in these moral codes.

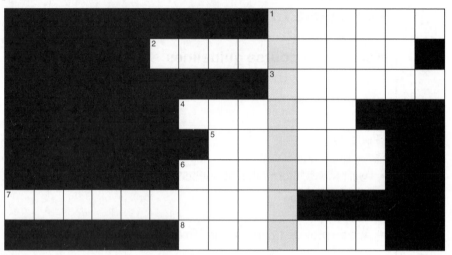

1 principles based on achieving perfection

2 minimum requirements marking a level of quality; a benchmark

3 a set of principles that people use to decide what is right/wrong

4 basic beliefs about what is right and morally good, that influence the way people behave

5 beliefs that determine whether something is important or not

6 ideas that people believe in and are certain are true

7 standards of character and behaviour

8 behaviour/habits that are expected and have been kept for a long time

2 Complete the famous quotes/moments from history using the words from exercise 1. You may need to change the form of the words to make it fit grammatically. The first letter has been done for you.

1 *'In law a man is guilty when he violates the rights of others. In e................ he is guilty if he only thinks of doing so.'*

Immanuel Kant 1724–1804, German philosopher

2 *'Strength and wisdom are not opposing v....................'*

Bill Clinton 1946– , Ex-president of the USA

3 *'A b................ is not merely an idea the mind possesses; it is an idea that possesses the mind.'*

Robert Oxton Bolt 1924–1995, English playwright and a two-time Oscar winning screenwriter

4 Archimedes is most famous for jumping out of a bath and shouting 'eureka' when he realised that the amount of water that overflowed from it was the same as his body weight. This 'displacement theory' is now known as *'Archimedes' P................'* .

Archimedes 287 BCE–212 BCE, Sicilian mathematician, engineer and designer

5 *'Manners easily and rapidly mature into m....................'*

Horace Mann 1796–1859, American educator and social reformer
American, *Educator Quotes*

6   'Other times, other .c....................'

Italian proverb

7   'To be an .i................ guest, stay at home.'

Edgar Watson Howe 1853–1937, American journalist, author

8   'The quality of a leader is reflected in the .s.................... they set for themselves.'

Ray Kroc 1902–1984, the man who made McDonald's famous around the world

Language focus

Grammar reference on page 222 of the coursebook.

Substitution and ellipsis

1   For each of the <u>underlined</u> items 1–5 in the text below, <u>underline</u> the correct choice in the alternatives below the text.

> ### A sound future
>
> There are many ways to improve the futures of our children. Educating them about money matters from an early age is one of [1]<u>them</u>. [2]<u>Doing so</u> would mean that they have fewer financial problems when they grow up. [3]<u>Not doing so</u>, on the other hand, would have dire consequences. [4]<u>Such negligence</u> will lead to more problems with the global economy. However, we must also teach children that money alone will not make them happy. [5]<u>To do so</u> will ensure that they grow up to be well-balanced individuals.

1   the many ways/the futures

2   improving the futures/educating them

3   not improving the futures/not educating them

4   financial problems/not doing so

5   teaching children that/global economy

2   Write the parts of the following sentences that are being left out or replaced. The word(s) to be replaced are in italics.

Example: There are many important lessons in life. Learning about the value of money is one of them. .One of the most important lessons in life...............

1   Tony bought a new car whereas Mike purchased a second-hand *one*. ....

2   Students often end up borrowing more money than they can afford. *Such actions* should be avoided if they want to avoid large sums of debt. ....

3   Jane called Mary. She did *so* to check that she was OK. ....

4   I looked after my sisters when they were young. I continue *to do so* even though they are not any more. ....

5   I read novels for pleasure but journals for facts. ....

6   Finding a job is much more difficult nowadays than *it was* in the past. ....

7   Some people say that education should be free for all though others criticise *such ideas* as unrealistic. ....

8   Although I wanted to finish this earlier, I was not able *to do so*. ....

Reading

You should spend about 20 minutes on **Questions 1–13**, which are based on the reading passage below.

A Everybody loves a pay rise. Yet over the past half-century, as developed economies have got much richer, people do not seem to have become happier. Surveys suggest that, on average, people in the USA, Europe and Japan are no more pleased with their lot than in the 1950s. This is curious, because at any given time richer people say they are happier than poorer people do. For instance, 37% of the richest quarter of North Americans claim to be 'very happy', compared with only 16% of the poorest quarter. That might lead you to expect that, as a country grows richer and incomes rise, rich and poor alike would become happier. However, they have not. Here lies a paradox: an individual who becomes richer becomes happier; but when society as a whole grows richer, nobody seems any more content.

B In recent years the study of 'happiness' — as opposed to more conventional economic measures, such as GDP per head — has attracted increased attention from economists. In a series of lectures earlier this year, Richard Layard, an economics professor at the London School of Economics, reviewed the various evidence from psychology, sociology and his own discipline to try to solve this paradox. One explanation is 'habituation': people adjust quickly to changes in living standards. So although improvements make them happier for a while, the effect fades rapidly. For instance, thirty years ago central heating was considered a luxury; today it is viewed as essential.

C A second and more important reason why more money does not automatically make everybody happier is that people tend to compare their lot with that of others. In one striking example, students at Harvard University were asked whether they would prefer (a) $50,000 a year while others got half that or (b) $100,000 a year while others got twice as much. A majority chose (a). They were happy with less, as long as they were better off than others. Other studies confirm that people are often more concerned about their income relative to others' than about their absolute income. Pleasure at your own pay rise can vanish when you learn that a colleague has been given a much bigger one. The implication of all this is that people's efforts to make themselves happier by working harder in order to earn and spend more are partly self-defeating: they may make more money, but because others do too, they do not get much happier. The unhappiness that one person's extra income can cause to others, argues Lord Layard, is a form of pollution.

D Worse still, working harder in order to be able to afford more material goods could even end up making people unhappier if they do not have enough spare time. Although people value their income in relation to that of others, this does not seem to be true of their leisure time. The same Harvard students were also asked to choose between (c) two weeks' holiday, while others have only one week and (d) four weeks' holiday while others get eight. This time a clear majority preferred (d). In other words, people's rivalry over income does not extend to leisure. The result of this, suggests Lord Layard, is that developed societies may tend to work too hard in order to consume more material goods, and so consume too little leisure.

E If governments' ultimate goal is to maximise the well-being (i.e. 'happiness') of society as a whole, then, says Lord Layard, some highly controversial implications for public policy follow. Conventional economic theory argues that taxation distorts the choice between leisure and income. Taxes reduce the incentive to work an extra hour rather than go home, or to put in extra effort in the hope of promotion. But Lord Layard's argument implies that people have a tendency to work too much. Far from being distortionary, taxes are therefore desirable. He suggests a marginal tax rate of 30% to deal with the 'pollution' that one person's extra income inflicts on others, and the same again for habituation. The total of 60% is a typical European level of taxation (taking both direct and indirect taxes into account).

F This flies in the face of what most economists think about high European taxes. In the USA, workers are allowed to keep more of the income from an extra hour's work. Many economists think that this is why Americans work longer hours than Europeans. Over the past two decades average annual working hours have increased slightly in the USA, but fallen sharply in Europe; continental Europeans now work, on average, 15% fewer hours than North Americans do. High taxes, it is argued, have undermined Europe's competitive edge. Lord Layard's analysis suggests an alternative view: it is not that Europeans are working too little, but that Americans work too long, driven to choose more income instead of leisure by an urge to keep up with the Joneses. Higher taxes in Europe encourage workers to choose more leisure rather than work, and so keep this urge in check. The United States' economic performance is superior if judged by GDP alone. But GDP is a flawed measure of economic well-being. Happiness demands leisure as well as material consumption. Americans may be richer than Europeans, but are they any happier?

G Seductive stuff, especially when read in August in a Tuscan villa or on a Mediterranean beach. Yet even if Lord Layard's theory is right, his figure for the optimal tax rate looks like little more than convenient guesswork. A lower number might be just as good. And Europe's high taxes still have negative effects. They put some people off working altogether, and discourage employers from offering extra jobs. As Lord Layard himself says, unemployment visits terrible unhappiness on those it afflicts. Yet this is not to deny his main point: the pursuit of material comforts does not always lead to happiness.

Questions 1–5

The reading passage has seven paragraphs, **A–G**.

Which paragraph contains the following information?

1 an example of a past indulgence that is now considered necessary in homes

2 the attitudes of students to spare time

3 something that all people agree is great to receive

4 another reason why receiving more money does not necessarily equal increased satisfaction

5 differences in work patterns and tax systems on two continents

Questions 6–9

Do the following statements agree with the information given in the Reading passage?

Write:

TRUE   if the statement agrees with the information

FALSE   if the statement contradicts the information

NOT GIVEN   if there is no information on this

6 Recently, economists have shown less interest in what constitutes happiness.

7 People do not compare the value of their holidays as they do their income.

8 According to Lord Layard, paying more taxes could be seen as a good thing as it keeps a population happier.

9 According to the author, the main reason for unemployment in Europe is the tax system.

Questions 10–13

Complete the sentences below.

Choose **NO MORE THAN TWO WORDS** from the passage for each answer.

10 Results seem to indicate that, on three continents, people are not happier with .... in comparison to the past.

11 Harvard University students were content with having less only if they were .... than other people.

12 In order to improve a nation's happiness, governments would have to implement some .... new policies.

Question 13

Choose the correct letter, **A**, **B**, **C** or **D**.

13 Which of the following is the most suitable title for the reading passage?

    A A paradox with an answer

    B How life is better in Europe

    C The secret of happiness

    D Why competition brings happiness

Writing

1 Read the Task 1 question below.

WRITING TASK 1

You should spend about 20 minutes on this task

The charts illustrate the results of a world online survey on optimism and happiness conducted in 2005.

Summarise the information by selecting and reporting the main features, and make comparisons where necessary.

Write at least 150 words.

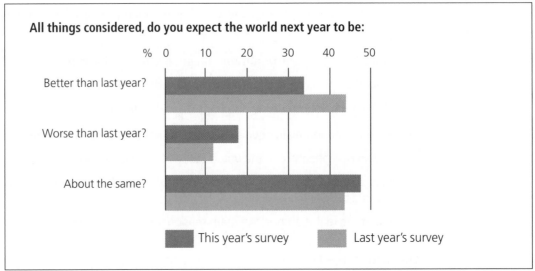

All things considered, do you expect the world next year to be:

This year's survey   Last year's survey

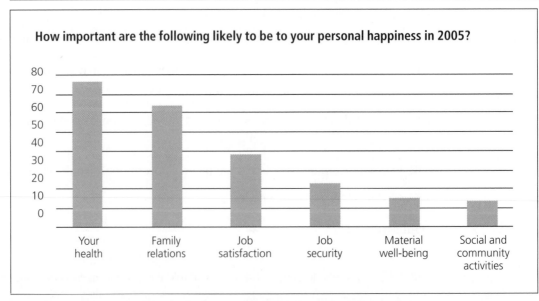

How important are the following likely to be to your personal happiness in 2005?

2   Use the instructions in the flow-chart to help you write your own answer.

> **1** What do the graphs show? Paraphrase the title to help you.

↓

> **2** Write an overview or say what the most striking feature is – do not include any specific data here!

↓

> **3** Compare the results in the first graph with the results from the year before. Write about each category separately. Sometimes use percentage as the subject of the clause and to avoid repetition, at other times use other 'quantity' words. (i.e. 'Thirty-five per cent of people...'/'The majority...') Write concession clauses to help you contrast effectively.

↓

> **4** Use a linking phrase to say that you are moving to the second chart. Start with the most popular response. Give the specific figure to support your sentence. (Use % as the subject of this sentence, as in the example above.)

↓

> **5** Go to the second most popular. Compare it to the first using substitution to avoid repetition. Support the information with data but round it up/down.

↓

> **6** Group all the ones to do with 'job' together and describe generally what is shown.

↓

> **7** Compare the last two.

↓

> **8** If you can think of something to say to round off, do. Otherwise, end your answer here.

3   When you have finished, check the following:

- content – have you answered the question fully?
- organization and cohesion – with the corrections, is your answer easy to read?
- range – have you used a wide range of vocabulary and grammar?
- accuracy – have you checked your spelling?

Listening scripts

1 We are all friends now

 1.1

(**J** = Julie; **M** = Mike)

J: Hi Mike! It's Julie. Listen, I know you're really busy, but we need to book our travel insurance. We're leaving in a couple of days after all.

M: Yeah sure. <u>I'm on my lunch break</u>, so go ahead!

J: OK, well my first question is what type of insurance do we need? I wasn't sure which to choose. Do we want the bronze, silver, gold or platinum type of policy?

M: What's the difference?

J: Well the first only covers medical expenses, the second covers medical and our baggage, and the gold all of that plus cancellation, and the platinum covers everything, including legal expenses.

M: OK, well if we're travelling in two days' time, we don't really need the cancellation policy, do we? What do you think?

J: Well, personally, the only thing that's really necessary is the medical cover.

M: Yeah, but would you think that if you had everything stolen?

J: Yeah, maybe you're right. Let's get the gold.

M: Sorry, don't you mean the silver? I thought we agreed that we don't need the cancellation cover.

J: <u>Oh yeah. You're right. Silver it is.</u>

M: So, how much is that going to cost us?

J: Well, there are two of us so let's see … it's … £25 for single cover and <u>£40 for a group of up to three people</u>.

M: But there are only two of us.

J: I know, but it's still cheaper than doing two individual policies. That would cost £50.

M: OK. Group cover it is.

J: Right, now, how are we going to pay? If we pay by debit card, there'll be a five per cent discount but I only have a credit card and there's a two and a half per cent charge for that. They don't have an office in central London so we can't pay by cash.

M: Oh really? What a pain!

J: <u>OK, well, I'll just have to use my credit card then.</u>

M: Great. That's sorted then. What else is there?

J: Well, you know that new expensive camera you bought and you were hoping to take some great pictures with?

M: Yes …

J: Well, the policy only covers equipment up to the value of £200 and didn't you say it cost £1000?

M: <u>No, I bought it for $1000.</u>

J: Yeah, but that's still more than £200 isn't it?

M: Well at the time that was around £500 but it's worth less than that now, maybe only £300.

J: So … to cover it you'd need to pay extra.

M: Mmm …

....

J: I just need to check your personal details to complete this online form and then we'll be sorted.

M: OK. What do you need to know?

J: Firstly, I need to make sure I've got your full name. It's Mike Wood, right?

M: Yep.

J: Right … , next I need your address.

M: It's <u>17 Hanley Gardens</u>, Hanley spelt H–A–N–L–E–Y.

J: Just writing that down … 17 Hanley Street …

M: No, Gardens!

J: Oops! My mistake! OK, what's your date of birth?

M: That's <u>23.07.70</u>.

J: Right, so now I need an emergency contact number. It's your mobile right?

M: Yes, it's <u>0793 245 098</u>.

J: Was that 0–8–9?

M: No, 0–9–8. Anything else?

J: Well, they need the main policy holder. Who would that be?

M: I think that would be you, since you're paying for it with your card.

J: Of course! So I just type in Julie <u>Bennett</u>… Hang on just typing B–E–N–N–E–T–T. OK, we're just about done. All I need to do is enter the dates of departure and return.

M: Well, we leave on Friday, which is the 16th.

J: No it isn't. It'll be the 17th.

M: Are you sure? Let me check my calendar … Oh yes, the 17th.

J: Right, so Friday <u>the 17th of July</u> and returning on Friday the 31st.

M: Hang on; if we fly out on Friday the 31st in the evening, it'll be the morning of Saturday the 1st by the time we get back with the time difference. We don't want our policy to run out before we land now, do we?

J: No, we don't! OK, so return date is Saturday <u>the 1st of August</u>. OK, my goodness that certainly took longer than I expected it to. I hope our trip is worth it!

M: Trust me Julie, you'll love it there, especially as you'll have your own personal guide.

J: Yes, OK. See you in a couple of days then. Bye!

M: See ya!

2 Technology – now and then

 1.2

Could I have your attention please … gather round, gather round. My name is Patricia and I'll be your guide around The Sydney Observatory. Now, as you all will know, man has been interested in the night sky for a very long time. <u>Indeed, before the invention of the compass, it was used by sailors to navigate their way across the world's oceans</u>, a kind of 'star' map you could say.

Now the site of the museum on Observatory Hill has its own interesting story. Before the colonizers arrived, it belonged to the Cadigal people, who may have even viewed the arrival of the new visitors from here, as this is the highest natural point in Sydney Harbour. <u>The early Europeans then built a windmill</u> on the site though it didn't last for long due to its exposed position. A little while after that, the land was used to build a fort, which was to finally become the observatory that you see before you today.

Now, let's take a look inside. <u>To the left of the main entrance is the cloakroom where you can leave your coats and bags, but please make sure you don't leave any mobiles or valuables as staff cannot be held responsible.</u> The museum is open during the day until 5 pm, so please collect belongings no later than 5.15 <u>and please vacate the building by 5.30</u>. No new admissions will be allowed after 4.30 pm. After you've left your personal items, you'll need to buy your tickets from the ticket desk immediately behind you, before continuing on the rest of the tour. The normal price is $8 for an adult and $6 for a child, <u>though groups of up to four people can save money by buying a family ticket. This must contain at least one adult and one child but no more than two children per adult.</u> I'll wait for you on the other side of the ticket barrier by the coffee shop, while you all get your ticket.

....

So, I hope you enjoyed the tour but before I leave you I just want to draw your attention to one more thing. <u>Your Observatory ticket also entitles you to visit another of Sydney's famous sights at a 50% discount.</u> You'll find lots on to keep the children entertained. For example, they've got sound workshops where you can have a go at being a DJ. <u>This is called the Soundhouse, and you'll find it up on the second floor, just after the kid's playground.</u> Look for signs for the Vectorlab workshops if you get lost. <u>For those of you interested in fashion and design, the Lace Study Centre should not be missed.</u> You'll get the chance to look at one of the country's best collections all in one place. However, like most museums, only a fraction of their collections are actually on display, <u>but in the museum's unique Discovery Centre,</u> you can take the opportunity to go behind the scenes and see parts of the collection that are not on display. <u>All of these attractions can be found under one roof at Sydney's famous Powerhouse museum.</u> I do hope you are able to go and enjoy the experience. You won't be disappointed!

3 Thrill seekers

 1.3

(**T** = Therese; **S** = Simon)
T: Hey Simon. You look down. How are you getting on with your essay for Professor Jones?
S: <u>Not very well I'm afraid. I can't seem to get my head around it. I mean, it's such a wide topic that I really haven't got a clue where to start.</u>
T: Oh poor you! I'm actually free now so I can give you a hand if you like? You have until the end of this week, don't you?
S: Yeah, I have to hand the essay in on Friday afternoon, but the Professor wants to see my proposal on Wednesday morning!
T: Today is Tuesday so that's tomorrow! You had better get a move on! Let's have a look.
S: Thanks. I'm just trying to brainstorm some ideas, but I haven't got very far.
T: Let me see … <u>Well firstly, I think that writing your ideas in a list like that really isn't going to help.</u> Remember how we were taught to do Spidergrams at the beginning of the year?
S: Diagrams?
T: No, not diagrams, SPIDERgrams! It's supposed to mimic the way our brains process information rather than simply expecting them to come out in some kind of logical order. They're also sometimes called Spidergraphs because of how they look, like a spider!

S: OK, I'll start over again.
T: Right, now our essay is on people's motivation for participating in extreme sports. There are two sides to this really; the external and internal influences.
S: Right, so let's look at the external influences first of all.
T: So what kind of things make people want to do extreme sports?
S: Well, the first thing that comes to mind is the amount of <u>media</u> attention on the topic. There are always stories about people taking part in the latest craze.
T: Exactly. Now let's think about this more carefully. Why does so much appear in the media?
S: I don't know. I've never really thought about it.
T: Well, according to the published materials out there, it's a reflection of modern <u>culture</u>.
S: Of course. Yes, you're right.
T: Now, what about the factors that come from within the person?
S: I suppose the most obvious thing to say is the adrenalin rush.
T: Right, but what else?
S: People would want to test their limits, which is a <u>psychological</u> need that all humans have.
T: And there's one more thing that we haven't added yet.
S: What's that?
T: What all animals do naturally: compete of course!
S: Right! It's the element of <u>competition</u> that drives all things to be the best! Now why didn't I think of that before?

....

T: How much background reading have you done on the topic?
S: Actually, none at all – it's really bad isn't it, but I just haven't had the time with my part-time job.
T: I know what you mean, but, honestly, it's so much easier once you've read around the topic a bit. Did you get a copy of the suggested sources, because if not I've got one here?
S: No, I didn't. Thanks, that's a great help.
T: I tell you what. You write down the main points and I'll read it out.
S: OK, go for it!
T: The first one's by a guy called Hans German and it's called *Crossing Borders*. It's a research project that was carried out on around <u>200 participants</u> of extreme sports. It's a really interesting read.
S: OK, what next?
T: The next book was written by a man called Richard Bell and is called *Motivation Theories*. It gives an overview of thrill seeking and why people choose to put their lives in danger.
S: Is it long?

T: Yeah, it's quite weighty, why?
S: It's just I really don't have very long before the essay needs to be in, so is there anything on there that would help me more quickly?
T: Well, I did find a podcast on the topic. I didn't write down the author's name, but they are called *The Mind Files* and it's also about the theories and principles but obviously doesn't go into as much detail as in a book.
S: That's absolutely fantastic Therese! How can I ever repay you?
T: Oh, I don't know … a coffee maybe?
S: Of course, my treat!

4 Global problems and opportunities

 1.4

Shall we start? Right, now … where did we get to last week? Ah, that's right, we were going to begin with a look at three of the world's most pressing problems; what has caused them as well as looking at some of the many possible solutions.

Top of the list is air, <u>water and soil</u> pollution. With an ever increasing demand for food, came the increased use of chemical pesticides during the late 1960s. Now, some of you may say that this isn't the ultimate root of the problem, overpopulation is, but you would be missing out a very important step. The increase in population didn't in itself lead to the pollution of the air, water and soil. What caused the problem in the first place was a move away from <u>traditional farming</u> methods, thanks to advances in technology. Ironically, the answer comes from past farming practices. Well, thankfully, the revolution has already begun. <u>Organic farming</u>, and a respect for nature's cycles, is the key to solving the problem.

In second place, though inextricably linked to the first issue, is the problem of the <u>natural resource</u> depletion. By that I mean, not only fossil fuels such as oil, coal and gas, but things we all too often take for granted, like fresh water and essential trace minerals in good quality soil. The main culprit, or guilty party, here is wasteful past <u>management practices</u> from those in power. Even though we knew that there were only finite supplies of traditional energy sources, we behaved like we didn't. The phrase that springs to mind is 'ignorance is bliss'. But what about a solution? Again, the process has already begun. We need to invest in new, less-polluting technologies in our vehicles – which will also help with the first problem – and use more hydrogen technology; that is, produce car engines that run on water. That's the way forward here. Not good drinking water, of course, but saline water, which is in abundance.

Finally, we come to the last problem, that of unequal wealth distribution. Every year, more and more land on the planet is owned by fewer and fewer people, which is in direct contrast to the world's growing population. And the reason for this? Quite simply, the greed and corruption of those in power, I'm afraid. The only way to solve this one, and it's a biggie, is for the countries of the world to work together in solidarity rather than against each other in isolation.

Now, although the solutions I have presented are viable, it doesn't mean that they're without their own potential problems. Firstly, making these kinds of changes is going to be expensive in the short-term, as we invest in the research and development of new technologies. Secondly, there's also the issue of popularity. It's the politicians of the world who need to make these changes, but they also need to keep their voters happy and may be reluctant to bring in new practices that may prove unpopular among voters at election time. But the biggest, and most important challenge, is making the world's monetary system fairer, by making things more equal and balanced for all. This includes adopting ecological practices that benefit all, not just a company's profit sheet. We need to begin an age of Corporate Social Responsibility, only then can we truly move forward.

5 The future

 1.5

(**H** = helpdesk worker; **C** = customer)
H: Good morning. How can I help?
C: I'd like some help with ordering a book. I've tried your website, but it says it's offline at the moment and to call this number.
H: Oh yes. I do apologize. We've been having some problems with it, but I can take the order over the phone if you like.
C: That would be great. It's a gift you see.
H: Can I take your name please?
C: Yes, of course. It's Zara Freeman.
H: Is that Zara with an 's' or a 'z'?
C: With a 'Z'. Z–A–R–A.
H: Just writing that down. Right. What was the title of the book you'd like me to order?
C: I think it's called *Future Words* … no hang on, sorry that's *Future Worlds*.

H: OK, just typing that in … I can't seem to find it. Do you know the name of the author? I'll do a search.
C: Yes, it's by a man called Richard Watson.
H: Watson as in W–A–T–S–O–N?
C: Yes, that's right.
H: Oh yes, here it is. It's only just been released. It's a self-help book. Is that right?
C: Yes.
H: Now, it costs £12.99.
C: Yep, that's fine.
H: OK. How would you like to pay?
C: Is a debit card OK?
H: No, sorry. We only accept credit cards.
C: Oh dear … Erm, Just let me check to see if I have it with me … Oh yes, here it is.
H: Can you read me the …

....

H: Right almost done. Now, I just need the delivery details.
C: Right. I've got my friend's address here. It's 62 Green Gardens, London N22.
H: Just typing that in … 52 Green Gardens.
C: No, it's number 62.
H: Now what kind of delivery would you like?
C: What are the options?
H: There are two. The free delivery option takes five days or you can pay an extra £2.25 to have it sent out first class tomorrow. That would come to a total of £15.24.
C: Umm … Well my friend's birthday is next week, so it should get there in time with the free delivery so I think I'll take that.
H: Right. That means that it will be delivered on the 21st February anytime from 8 am to 6 pm Is that OK?
C: Well, I know my friend leaves early for work, so would it be possible for him to pick it up from the local post office instead?
H: I'm afraid that won't be possible but I could add some special instructions for it to be left with someone else, a neighbour perhaps?
C: Actually, yes. I have met the old lady who lives next door and she's bound to be home. Could you leave it with her?
H: Fine. I'll add that if he's not home then the package should be left with the neighbour.
C: That's great! Thanks very much for your help.
H: My pleasure. Thank you for …

6 Fruits and seeds

 1.6

Welcome to the Homes of the Future online website. I will be your virtual guide around the homes you could soon be living in. Let's begin our tour in the bedroom. Firstly, the bed is programmed to gently rock you awake in the mornings. There'll be no more rude awakenings by an alarm clock, and it will also know what time you need to wake up as it will get that information directly from your Personal Digital Assistant, that is, your PDA, which will be inserted into you.

Let's move to the wardrobe. Those are your musical shoes that generate music while you walk. The music will change according to how fast you're walking; calm music for a relaxing stroll and faster beats for when you're in a hurry. You'll feel like you're walking on air. What's more, your clothes are also intelligent. They sense how you're feeling and then change colour. The fabric that they're made of also converts your body heat into a low-voltage electricity generator for some of the gadgets that are now inside you, like your PDA, for example.

Moving on to the bathroom … So, after waking up, you need a shower. There's no need to turn on any taps as the house will know exactly what temperature you like the water in the mornings, though you'll still have to wash yourself!

From the bathroom, we move into the kitchen. Now, we've all had that horrible feeling when you can't find your keys just as you're about to go out. Well, in the home of the future you wouldn't need to panic, all you need to do is an Internet search. All items are now programmed with a tracking device so that they will light up and signal to you where they are. Just in case the object is upstairs, the house will project its position on your fridge.

Speaking of your fridge, this is now as intelligent as your clothes. Not only does it keep a record of when you're running low on everyday essentials like milk, but it emails your local grocery store, which will deliver them for you. It can also help with planning meals if you have friends over for dinner by moving the chicken from the freezer so that it'll thaw in time.

....

Lastly, here we are in the living area, which, you'll be pleased to hear, is still the heart of the family home. Let's enter the room. Now, to the left of the entrance is the main seating area with a sofa, and directly opposite the entrance is an armchair. The sofa backs onto the wall and the armchair faces to the left, across the coffee table to a blank wall. So, 'where is the TV?' I hear you ask. Well, this entire wall is the television. The whole thing is a plasma screen designed to show your TV, surf the Internet or, when it's not in use, it displays anything you want it to from family pictures to famous works of art.

On the opposite wall to the sofa is a fireplace, which still has a real fire – nothing beats that now, does it? But the rug in front of the fire now also monitors the temperature, and either opens or closes the chimney, so as not to overheat the room. It still has its normal uses though, as you can see, the cat likes it very much and is curled up on it, happy as can be.

What else is on offer? Well, for entertainment the family still reads books, so there is a bookcase on the wall to the right of the entrance. But what about the computer? Well, it's inside your head and powered by those intelligent clothes you're wearing. Imagine this: as you're sitting relaxing on the armchair, you'll be able to reach out and put your hot drink on the coffee table in front of the armchair. You suddenly remember that you need to send work an email. That same coffee table holding your cup is also a touch sensitive keyboard for you to type your email and then click 'send'. All you need to do to activate it is say 'email' and the image of a keyboard will appear.

Well, I hope you've enjoyed your tour around the home of the future and that you'll come visit again soon. Bye-bye.

7 The world of work and training

 1.7

(**S** = Sally; **P** = Professor James)
S: Hi Professor James, have you got a minute? You see I'm having a bit of trouble getting started on my graduate employability assignment.
P: Well, OK, as long as it doesn't take longer than ten minutes as I have a meeting to get to at 3.30.
S: Yep fine. It shouldn't take long at all.
P: OK, Sally. Tell me what you've done so far and we'll go from there.
S: Well, as you suggested I chose three local businesses and contacted them via telephone to introduce myself.
P: That's good.
S: Well, the thing is, I couldn't get past the secretary of two of them. Do you have any suggestions?
P: What about following up with a letter stating what time you'll be calling again?

S: Oh, that's a good idea. I hadn't thought of that.
P: So, tell me about the one you have contacted.
S: Right, well, he was very helpful actually. He received the survey I emailed him and has already sent it back. I've had a very quick look at it, but haven't had a chance to write it up yet.
P: So far so good. Carry on ...
S: Well, apart from that, I've also found a lot of statistics that exist on the starting salaries graduates begin on once they finish studying. There's some really interesting stuff out there. Did you know, for example, that your average engineer earns nearly as much as a medical graduate?
P: Yes, I did.
S: Gosh, I had no idea.
P: Having second thoughts about a career in human resources are we?
S: No, but I was surprised. Anyway, getting back to where I was. I've gone to the library, but the books you recommend have already been taken out, apart from one that is, it's called ... *A Starting Success*. I haven't read it yet, but I've taken it out and it's on my list of things to do.
P: Have you come up with a plan yet?
S: Yes, and I've written my hypothesis as well as my introduction, but that's where I've got stuck. I don't really know how I'm going to be able to present all of the information as there's so much of it ...

....

P: Well firstly, I'd recommend you start with analyzing what the employer said. Now can I have a look at the questionnaire you wrote?
S: Yes, here it is.
P: Thanks ... Oh dear. Well it's no wonder you're overwhelmed with information. You've collected a lot of information, which can be overwhelming.
S: Oh dear! That took me ages... and does that mean I can't use it?
P: Afraid so ... but don't worry if you've got a pen and paper, I'll quickly give you some pointers, and then you can re-jig it to get the information you're looking for.
S: OK, just a minute ... I know there's a pen in here somewhere. OK, got it.
P: Right, well, first and foremost you need to be clear. There's no point having a beautifully worded document throughout that no one understands. Use language that is simple.
S: Right, got that. What next?
P: You need to catch the reader's attention at the start of the

document. And you need to find the right balance between formal and informal language. Your survey isn't an official document, but more of a living one that serves a purpose, so neutral language is best.
S: OK, just writing that down ... OK.
P: The next one's what your mistake was this time – try not to use open-ended questions, or you'll find it impossible to collate your results.
S: Yep, I think I've learned my lesson there. What else?
P: Scales really do make the job of completing the questionnaire easier for the recipients by saving them lots of time and effort writing.
S: I take your point. Anything else?
P: Ah ha. One last thing. Make sure you've thought about the logic of your questions. There's nothing worse than trying to make choices about things that seem to have no order.
S: Right ... got it. I see where I went wrong now and will try to do better next time.
P: Don't worry. It's a very easy mistake to make, and one that many people come across the first time they do this kind of assignment. OK, Sally, I really must rush. I'm late for my appointment.
S: Of course, thanks for your help. I'll see you in class tomorrow. Bye!

8 The history of geography

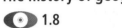 1.8

Hi, good morning everyone. I'm here today to present my findings on the process of urbanization and its impact on the environment. As you know, urbanization involves the movement of people from the countryside to the cities. As this process continues, the cities of the world continue to grow. I will demonstrate how this growth is eating away at the planet's most fertile land.

My research has focused on two studies that looked at land use in the United States. These have shown that since its independence, only three per cent of all land in the United States has been built on. However, the same studies have also shown that the resulting loss of productive land is comparatively much, much greater. This isn't so much of a problem in America as it has a relatively low ratio of people to land. However, most other countries are not so blessed, the impact of which could have dire consequences for the future. The real danger here is if this pattern were to be repeated by developing countries, it could have a major effect on the world's food supplies in the next 50 years.

In order to reach this conclusion, several research methods were adopted. A group of scientists in the United States used a weather <u>satellite</u> that normally maps moonlit cloud cover at night. However, on nights when there were no clouds, they used the satellite to map the generation of heat from city lights. They then took the data and divided land use into <u>three categories</u>: urban, semi-urban and non-urban land use. Next, they calculated how active the vegetation is in each region by using different satellites. When they combined this information with previous statistics and weather conditions, they came up with a number for <u>total productivity</u> for all areas.

....

So what did the results of this process of land classification show? Well, firstly, they proved that although only a tiny percentage of the land in the United States is urbanized, and 29 per cent of land is used for agricultural purposes, the land which has been built on actually has the <u>best soils</u>. These were independently corroborated by a second team of scientists in San Francisco, whose results show that this process is happening even faster in the south-eastern corner of the United States. This means that land that is extremely productive from an agricultural point of view, is being taken over by lawns, golf courses and a few scattered trees. As a direct result of urbanization, the researchers in San Francisco calculated that every year <u>91 million tonnes</u> of plants are 'lost' in the U.S.

So what does this mean for the future? Well, I have come up with some of my own ideas for practical solutions. Countries should calculate whether urbanization is happening on their fertile lands too; especially if they have large populations compared to the amount of land available, like <u>India</u> and <u>China</u>, for example. If it is, then every effort should be made to stop the process from happening. This can be done in many ways. One of them is to stop investing in the infrastructure of those areas. If people don't have the facilities they need, they won't want to live there. But in my opinion, the main solution here is to offer people <u>financial incentives</u> to move away from fertile land to areas that are less valuable in agricultural terms.

I hope you've enjoyed my presentation this morning. Thanks for your kind attention. I will now take any questions …

9 What is beauty?

 2.1

(**A** = Anna; **C** = Chris)

A: Hi Chris! What are you doing here? I thought you were supposed to be revising for your finals in the library?

C: Yeah, well I decided it was time for a break. I really wasn't being very productive so thought I'd come and have a coffee and some fresh air to see if that'd help. What are you doing with all those prospectuses?

A: Well I'm trying to decide which university to apply to for my MA in Music. The choice is really overwhelming!

C: Well that certainly is a big pile of prospectuses. Maybe talking about it will help you at least narrow it down? I've got some time, and to be honest, it'll be a welcome distraction from my dissertation.

A: Great! Thanks Chris. So far, the universities that appeal the most are The Academy in London, Leeds Conservatory of Contemporary Music and The Henry Music Institute , which is also in London.

C: I'm not an expert but wouldn't <u>The Henry Music Institute</u> be the best as it's the one that everyone's heard of?

A: Well … yes and no. Leeds Conservatory of Contemporary Music is also pretty famous and although The Academy in London is less well-known, they've got some excellent modules on offer.

C: But still, it's always good to have a well-known name on your CV, even if Leeds Conservatory of Contemporary Music and The Academy in London are good … What about the entry requirements? That might help you to make a decision.

A: Well, funny you should say that as I was just looking at them. The Academy in London requires an audition as does The Henry Music Institute.

C: Leeds Conservatory of Contemporary Music doesn't?

A: No, they want candidates to compose a piece of music instead, <u>before attending an interview.</u>

C: Don't the others require you to do that? Compose, that is?

A: No, the others ask you to write an assignment stating why you want to join the course first of all, but if I pass that stage then I'll also have to attend a face-to-face <u>interview</u> like the other two places with the head of school. Assuming that goes OK, then I'll be accepted onto the course.

C: Right. Sounds tough!

A: I know, but I suppose it's for a Master's degree so I wasn't expecting it to be easy.

C: What about the fees? Are they all the same?

A: Well, surprisingly, the fee structures are very different.

C: Why's that?

A: I really don't know, but, for example, The Henry Music Institute is the most expensive at £8,000 a year, next comes The Academy in London and the cheapest is Leeds Conservatory of Contemporary Music.

C: Mmm … How much are they exactly?

A: Well, for a full-time course lasting one year it's £7,000 at The Academy in London and <u>£6,000</u> at Leeds Conservatory of Contemporary Music.

C: OK. Well, what other expenses do you have to take into consideration, like train fares for example? If you're going to be travelling home and back during the holidays, that's got to be a factor.

A: I'm not worried about that, though insurance is an added cost as I'll need to make sure my instrument is covered. However, all of them require me to send in a cheque for the charges for applying before they'll process my <u>application</u>.

C: Is that normal?

A: Apparently …

C: Can I have a look?

A: Yes, of course. Here you are.

C: Ummmm.

A: What is it?

C: Well, I think you might have a problem.

A: Why? What is it?

C: Well it says here that the deadline is January the 9th. That's next week.

A: Where? Let me see … you're right! Which prospectus is this?

C: The Henry Music Institute …

A: Oh no! What am I going to do?

C: Make your decision now?

A: Is the closing date the same for all of them?

C: Let's check … Look here, Leeds Conservatory of Contemporary Music is on the 19th but The Academy in London isn't until the 30th of this month.

A: OK, I'd better hurry up and make a decision.

....

A: Right, now, apart from those three colleges I also wanted to have a quick flick through Northdown College's and the one from The James Academy of Music.

C: Look here it is; facilities at Northdown College.

A: What does it say?

C: Well, it has a library with a dedicated <u>historical research section</u> that's world famous.

A: That's all very interesting, but it's not going to make me go there.

C: OK, The Academy in London has <u>four campuses</u> all around central London. They all have large common rooms and there's one 24 hour cafeteria at the biggest site.

A: That's nice, but for me the most important thing is somewhere to practise.

C: Yes, of course.

A: Right, now where did I see it … OK, here it is. Look, now this is good. Leeds Conservatory of Contemporary Music has over 100 teaching and <u>practice studios</u>. What a luxury! Here there are only ten and it's really difficult to find one empty so I often have to play in the gardens.

C: Oh dear!

A: Anyway, that's the past and this place looks great!

C: Well what about The Henry Music Institute? Look, there's <u>a new suite with the latest that technology has to offer</u> and a small museum dedicated to the history of music. That's really impressive!

A: I don't think I'm really that interested in using computers while making music, so that's not a selling point really. But look, this place is interesting. The James Academy of Music. It comes recommended by lots of people in the music industry, and all of its courses have a business element as well as having <u>a professional studio for recording albums</u>.

C: Wow! That sounds really cutting-edge. So are you any closer to making a decision now?

Unit 10 Is it art?

 2.2

(**P** = Professor McKinley; **M** = Michael)

P: Hello everyone. Before we continue with our lectures on the history of music and art, we'll be listening to Michael's presentation on how music and art are being used to help with the healing process in the 21st century. Michael, are you ready to begin?

M: Yes, I think so … Thanks professor. Right. Good morning all. As Professor McKinley just stated, I've been doing some research into the healing powers of art and music, and I'd like to present my findings to you today. I intend to demonstrate the positive effects of music and art on patients' emotional, <u>social</u> as well as physical well-being.

Let's begin by going back in time to the most famous of nurses, Florence Nightingale. Way back in <u>1860</u>, Florence Nightingale wrote in her *Notes on Nursing* that brightly coloured flowers

and art helped her patients to recover more quickly. Although her comments were viewed with scepticism at the time, she was – we believe – the first of many health professionals to state this.

Over the following years, there were many other studies that tried to prove that a link between art, music and health exists, but very few of them were <u>strictly controlled</u>, so the results were variable, and therefore unreliable. However, one American study was different. In the 1980s, some research took place into the effects of architecture on the <u>recovery time</u> of 46 patients who were in hospital for a gall bladder operation. Half of the patients were kept in hospital wards with windows overlooking some trees. The other half were left in rooms that faced onto a brick wall. It was found that the ones with a <u>nice view</u> left hospital a day earlier and needed fewer painkillers. This study was groundbreaking as it was the first that used controlled conditions that could be measured statistically and without bias.

....

M: Now I'd like to bring you up-to-date and take a closer comparative look at three research projects on three very different types of patient. The first monitored the health of unborn babies. In the study, which took place at a hospital in London, babies were played <u>live music</u> and their heart rates were monitored. A healthy baby's heart would beat around 110 to 160 times a minute, but researchers found that their heart rate increased by up to 15 beats a minute on average without the mother's pulse changing. This is a good sign that the baby is healthy. In addition, the mothers that took part in the survey also said they felt more relaxed.

Another study looked at cancer patients who were visiting as day patients to receive their chemotherapy treatments. They were treated in a room that had <u>artistic pictures</u> hanging on the wall. The pictures were changed each week so that the patients would not have to look at the same ones week after week. When questioned afterwards, patients said that they <u>felt less pain</u> because the images helped take their mind off the treatment they were receiving. They also noted general improvements in their well-being.

Finally, the last study analyzed the treatment of a group of elderly patients who were in

hospital to have a hip replacement operation, and so they needed to stay for around 10–14 days. The researchers played them 30 minute tracks of <u>soothing classical music</u>, but not every day, and then monitored their progress using a questionnaire. When asked to rate how they felt both with and without music, the patients consistently stated that they felt less anxious on the days when they had the music playing. There was a second unexpected, but completely understandable result from the research. The staff liked the music so much that they said they too <u>felt happier</u> and that they would be less likely to leave the hospital for a job elsewhere if it were to continue. Now that has to be a good thing, which will also have a positive effect on the quality of the treatment patients receive.

In conclusion …

11 Psychology and Sociology

 2.3

(**K** = Katie; **R** = resident)

K: Hi, good afternoon sir, er … excuse me! Could you spare a minute please?

R: Oh, hello. Sorry, I was in a world of my own … I didn't hear you there.

K: No problem. My name's Katie and I'm a second year sociology student. We're doing a research project on the importance of <u>community centres</u> to local residents. May I ask, are you a resident of Molton?

R: Yes, I am.

K: That's perfect. Would you mind answering some questions about the facilities you use? It won't take very long …

R: Of course, I'd be happy to answer any questions you have. Fire away!

K: Great! OK, the first questions are to do with you. So can I ask how old you are? We need to know for statistical purposes later.

R: Well, I'd like to say 16 but I'm <u>59</u>, 60 next week in fact.

K: Congratulations for next week! Now I just need your postcode, and then we'll get started.

R: Right, well that's an easy one. It's H–A–8–7–U–P.

K: 7–A–8 … H–Q–P, was that right?

R: No my dear, it's <u>H–A–8–7–U–P</u>.

K: Right … OK. Sorry for the confusion.

R: That's quite alright. Now what about these questions?

K: Yes, let's get started … So one of the most important things we need to know is which of the facilities you already use.

R: Right OK.

K: OK, what about computer facilities? Do you currently use public computers anywhere in town?

R: Yes, I do. I go to my <u>local library</u>.

K: Great, … just jotting that down. OK, what about local sports facilities?

R: Yes, I get down to the <u>swimming pool</u> at least twice a week.

K: And education facilities? Are you currently attending any courses?

R: Yes, I go to Spanish classes every Friday at the <u>further education college</u>.

K: That's great! I must say, you're very active.

....

K: OK, we're halfway through. The next bit is all about how the community centre could be improved, if at all, that is.

R: I see. Well, I'll give it a go!

K: Well firstly, I'd like to find out your views on sports facilities. Which sports do you think the community centre should offer that it doesn't already?

R: Mmm … Well, I'm not going to say swimming as there's no point having two pools in a town of this size. Let me think … um, what about yoga? I know it's very popular these days. Yes, <u>yoga</u> and <u>badminton</u>. I used to play you know.

K: Really?

R: Yes, and I was quite good though I'm probably a bit rusty now. It's been years.

K: OK, do you think the classes should be split into groups?

R: Yes, that's a good idea. I know that if there were classes <u>only for pensioners</u>, I'd definitely be more likely to play. I'm not as fast as I once was, you know.

K: OK, I'll just write that down … Great! Now, we're nearly done. I just need to ask you some questions about education. What kind of classes do you think the centre should offer that it doesn't already?

R: Well, I suppose the kind of thing that's no longer offered at the local college, em … things like <u>arts</u> and <u>crafts</u>. Those kinds of classes have now closed as they weren't financially viable, apparently.

K: Yes, I heard about that. It was such a shame. Those kinds of classes are so important for the psychological well-being of those most vulnerable in a community. OK, I've written that down. Now, I need to ask you whether you would be willing to pay for any of the services we were just talking about.

R: Umm, as long as it wasn't too much, I have nothing against

contributing. Something like <u>two pounds per class</u> seems like a reasonable rate for an old man like me!

K: OK, em … and lastly then, I just need to know how regularly you think you will use the new facilities if the community centre makes the changes you have suggested.

R: Well, I'd say <u>three times</u> a week, which is more than I go at the moment. I only bother on Mondays and Wednesdays, as there's nothing else on during the week that interests me. But I would definitely get out of the house more if they were to make those kinds of changes.

12 Travelling around the world

 2.4

Hi and welcome to the walking audio tour service, which offers guided audio tours of over 30 walks around London. The full list of the walks is available on our website. You have chosen the Hampstead Heath Tour Part 1, which was, in fact, the first of the walking tours that were recorded. Your walk takes you through part of the heath, a <u>huge</u>, wild, open parkland where Londoners and visitors to the city can come and enjoy some leisurely and refreshing exercise. The heath is one of the gems of north London. When you enter the parkland, you will feel as if you are walking in the wild countryside, but you are actually still in an urban area.

The walking tour begins here at the exit to Hampstead underground station, <u>which is the deepest station on the London Underground system.</u> We hope that you enjoy your experience, whether you are on your own or sharing your walk with a companion … So let's begin your tour. We hope you enjoy it!

If you turn right as you exit Hampstead station, and stay on the right hand side of the road, the main thorough-fare, Heath Street, will take you up the hill to the heath itself. You are now walking away from the main shops and cafés in Hampstead village, <u>but you can return to visit these after your walking tour for some window shopping</u>. The village is busy during the daytime and the evenings.

Now back to Heath Street. As the road winds northwards up Heath Street, you will pass some shops and restaurants on your way to the heath. When you reach the top, the first part of the heath that you will see on your right is the Vale of the Heath, <u>which has some spectacular houses, built on the Heath itself beside a large pond</u>. If you go along a little further you will

come to a fork in the road, where one road – North End Way – turns to the left and goes northwest away from the heath; and on your right is Spaniards Road, which turns north-east, cutting through the parkland. Walk along this latter road a little way and look for the first opening on your right, where a path leads you down into the wild parkland.

As you descend along the pathway, you will find that the noise of the busy road, that is just on your left, disappears completely. <u>You might want to take off your headphones to enjoy the delight of the sounds of the parkland</u>. Don't imagine that there is only silence! There is the noise of the trees and the wildlife that lives there. As you walk along the path, you will come across several paths coming from the right to join the path that you are on, but keep going until you come to the first fork in the path. Now take the path that goes to your left, which will bring you shortly to the open spaces around Kenwood House.

....

You can either walk through the woods and enjoy being among the trees, or you can savour the other charms the heath has to offer. You are now at Kenwood House, which is a museum open to the public. It has been used as the setting for several well-known films, and is used as a venue for a wide range of functions. <u>For some light refreshments, there is the café at Kenwood House.</u> Below Kenwood House itself, you can see <u>the grassy slopes, which are an ideal place for picnics</u> and for children to run around and play games. Just beyond this picnic area is <u>an open air stage where music concerts are held in the</u> summer months. You might even see the stage being prepared for a concert while you are there.

You might want to explore this part of the heath at your leisure. But before you leave the heath altogether there are two other notable features that are worth visiting. On the east side of the heath are <u>several large ponds for segregated and mixed bathing</u>. And if you would like a view of London, you can visit Parliament Hill, which gives you <u>a good panorama of London</u> that is in fact protected by law.

13 The importance of infrastructure

 2.5

(**J** = Jack; **T** = tutor)

J: Hi! Am I bothering you? Is it OK to see you now?

T: Hi Jack! No bother. Please come

in. As your tutor this year, it's my responsibility to oversee your assignments. Now, where are my notes? Oh yes, here they are. OK, I see that we were going to look at your case study on the challenges of urban planning in the 21st century and how to make it as 'green' as possible. How's it all going?

J: Actually, I'm pretty happy with it. Can I talk you through it to make sure I'm on the right track?

T: Of course, please do. I'll stop you if I have any questions.

J: OK, well I started by giving an overview of what 'green' urban planning has been up until now. Firstly, there's the idea of a green belt. This is the one that everyone's heard of, but I found that while it was successful for a short time and in limited cases, it grossly oversimplified things.

T: Well that's a good and practical start. What else did you look at? I hope that you also considered the idea of decentralization?

J: Yes, that was really interesting, as although there were no objections to it and it looked good on paper, it just didn't work in practice.

T: Yes, a conundrum indeed. However, I think you'll find that there are many fads that come and go in this area. It isn't the first and it won't be the last to simply disappear off the face of the planet. Well this is all very good so far. What did you look at next?

J: I then researched the 1960s fad of building new towns on new sites, but I found that although there are isolated cases of success, they tended to cost too much time and money to build.

T: Keeping to that theme, have you considered the idea of brownfield sites? That is sites that previously had another use, being converted into residential areas?

J: Like the idea of buildings that were once banks being turned into restaurants? That kind of thing?

T: Yeah, that's right.

J: No, I hadn't thought of that.

T: Well, I'd say it's a pretty important option in most urban areas today. Even though there have been issues with safety, if the land were contaminated in any way, at least it tends to attract no objections from local residents.

J: OK, thanks. I'll make sure I put that in.

T: Anything else?

J: Well, I'm not sure about this last one, but I thought the idea of pedestrianizing central areas was an interesting concept. Do you think it's valid here?

T: Oh, it's certainly not a bad idea.

The only thing is that it would probably intensify the problem of congestion in inner city areas and would disrupt local residents' sleep, if the construction work were to happen during the night. The use of loud excavators to re-pave the area would be inevitable.

J: Yes, I take your point, but in some older cities, I think it's one of the few viable options.

T: Well as long as you state that, then it can definitely be included.

....

J: OK, so that's my introduction to urban planning sorted, but now I come to the main part, which is the case study. It was really difficult to choose as there are so many good examples, but in the end I settled on Curitiba, which is the capital of the south Brazilian state of Paraná.

T: Ah, yes. Nice choice. How's the research coming along?

J: Well, to be honest, I'm finding the amount of material a bit too much. There's such a diverse range of statistics that it makes it almost impossible to be selective.

T: Well, tell me a bit more about what you've discovered, and then we'll see if we can come up with a plan to tackle the problem.

J: Well, it's fascinating. Local authorities managed to achieve so much since the 1960s, principally because rather than waiting for central government initiatives they chose a cohesive strategy where residents were consulted. Then they took their ideas and implemented them into local government planning to come up with a plan everybody was happy with.

T: A ha! A bottom-up approach. Do go on …

J: Well, the transport system is a real example of the town's eco-friendly image. Even though they have one of the highest number of cars per person in the country, they also have the highest number of people using public transport. This is because poor and elderly residents are able to benefit from a social fare that allows them to use the system for less. This has led to low levels of pollution which also encourages citizens to use bicycles more.

T: Well, that's really impressive Jack. Well done. But I do have some suggestions to help you with finalizing your case study.

J: Please …

T: If you are going to prove Curitiba's success, you need to refer to specifics. You mentioned pedestrian only areas in your introduction, how about that?

J: Yes, OK.

T: And what about the amount of parking for all of those cars?

J: I didn't come across that in my research, but I can look it up.

T: Yeah, I think it's important.

J: And what about considering where people live in relation to their place of work? If they live in the suburbs, how about mentioning how far they need to travel in order to get to work?

T: And don't forget about their recycling strategy, including how easy it is and how much they recycle, making sure you include statistics to back it up.

J: OK, got it.

T: All in all Jack, you've really done your homework and I very much look forward to receiving your final draft.

J: Thanks professor. You've been a great help.

14 Money and happiness

 2.6

Good morning everyone and welcome to the Stanley University School of Economics. I will be one of your lecturers on the course and my name is Professor Whitefield. Before the academic year really gets underway, I would like to take you through some of what you can expect and to give you some general course information.

Firstly, you'll be attending lectures during which you will receive information about economics and the priorities that you will need to focus on. The lectures will provide you with information about the subject in a relatively condensed format. In addition, they should also provide a suitable framework for further study. Typically, this is also the first time that students get the chance to meet a researcher at the forefront of the discipline. Traditionally, lectures are seen as an essential part of the learning culture for higher education, in which undergraduate study is viewed as an induction into academic discipline and a way of viewing the world.

However, although all I have said until now is true, every year undergraduate students experience problems with the techniques used in lectures. Being forewarned will hopefully help you with adjusting to these issues. The first problem is that there is little opportunity for the development of student understanding. That is, if you misunderstand something, there is no immediate opportunity to ask. Secondly, when newer teaching approaches are used, such as problem-solving, learning outcomes are improved. However, these will still not replace the validity of listening and learning from an expert.

....

Now, before you start despairing there are several things that you can do in order to make the learning process, and consequently your student life at the university, easier.

First and foremost, be prepared! You will be given a reading list. Don't just throw it away or forget about it; make sure you leave enough time to go through all items on it. Once you've done that, an ideal thing to do would be to test yourself on the contents. Prepare a mini quiz while reading, and go back to it before the lecture and just check you know the answers. Now for most of you, this won't be the first time that you're studying economics, but you may have taken a gap year or had a period of time working. If this is so, and even if it isn't in fact, it always makes sense to go back and refresh your memory on those relevant theories you learned about before, as we'll definitely be referring to them.

OK. There're just a couple more ideas I'd like to suggest before I'll take any questions you may have. We are lucky enough to be living in a digital age, so use resources like the web to do some extra background research. There's no shortage of information nowadays, but just be sure that you're using reliable resources. Finally, and this is an important one: make sure you discuss ideas with your peers. They are in the same boat as you are after all, and you will probably find that it helps make your learning more memorable. All in all, take charge of your learning and you will find that you succeed. Now, do you have any questions before we go on to …

Wordlist

Write your own definitions on the lines provided to help build your vocabulary.

Unit 1

Reading

barrier

beneficial

bereavement

boost

build emotional bridges

companionship

crucial

enable

fitness

household

hunting

impact

labour

lengthy

regain

rejoin

supportive

unconditional

well-being

Writing Task 1

access

pace

soar

Unit 2

Reading

conquer

crude

culminate

devise

empirical

evolution

evolve

fertile

forefather

fundamental

lasting

momentous

nomadic

sake

succession

transition

trigger

utilise

vital

Writing Task 2

chore

cost-effective

ensure

fast-paced

mechanised

specialization

Unit 3

Reading

charge

dozens

exposure

found

humble

key

manoeuvrability

prestigious

primarily

rank

sprint

Writing Task 1

diversity

glamour

motivate

response

strategy

visual aspect

Unit 4

Reading

emissions

employ

entire

entirely

fossil fuel

generate

geothermal

grid

intermittent

plant

renewable

ridge

sparsely populated

switch

target

Writing Task 2

beneficial

financial incentive

inhabitant

Wordlist

labour force

latest

migrate

potential

productive

prospect

redress the balance

relocate

skilled

vital

Unit 5

Reading

accuracy

adopt (an approach)

analogous

analyse

comprehend

decode

detect

device

downstream

emphasise

ethical

figure out

imaginary

implication

index

precise

predict

randomly

reconstruct

rehabilitate

scanner

undergo

Writing Task 1

eightfold

hardly

historically speaking

significant

Unit 6

Reading

abnormality

breakthrough

conservationist

ecological

exceptionally

extract

frustration

handle

overcome

preserve

presumption

steadily

temperate

tolerant

tremendous

trickiest

tropical

uniform

variable

Writing Task 1

boil

condense

conventional

generate

pressure

pump

surface

Unit 7

Reading

applicable

breadth

component

corporate social responsibility

distinction

dry

dynamic

engaging

genuinely

implement

incorporate

integrated

interactive

leaning

recognition

slant

sound

sustainability

upshot

yawn

Writing Task 2

advance

assessment

efficient

exclusively

(a major) impact on (something)

memo

practical assessment

substantiate

Unit 8

Reading

alter

arise

biodiversity

capture

comprehensive

detrimental

devastate

disintegrate

disturb

ecosystem

expedition

exploit

glimpse

habitat

herd

induce

inventory

massive

pristine

remote

sample

seabed

unique

virgin

Writing Task 1

comparatively

considerable

infrastructure

investment

recreational

relatively

triple

Unit 9

Reading

attainable

attribute

bias

competence

conceit

concern

critical

dissatisfied

distorted

exceptional

excessive

indifferent

irrational

mass media

moral

praise

pride

progressively

resemble

rigid

self-esteem

severe

stereotype

uniform

vanity

vary

virtue

Writing Task 2

annoying

at the expense of

deliberately

pleasing to the eye

role

worthy

Unit 10

Reading

assured

bring about

culminate

dramatic

function

hover

intend

landscape

lighten

motive

myth

nonsense

observe

ostensible

passion

perceive

permanent

persist

portray

print

profound

refine

represent

stretch back

sustained

unquenchable

Writing Task 2

vital

well-rounded

Unit 11

Reading

addicted

adolescent

advances

approach

associate

break a habit

Wordlist

conserve

contaminating

crucial

depict

detect

(widely) disseminated

exploit

impending

inadvertently

ineffective

insight

kick in

lead

modify

nurture

offspring

resemble

revolution

unintended

virtually

Writing Task 2

consumer society

convince someone

material possessions

pursuit

short-lived

Unit 12

Reading

emerge

eternal

evocative

face

famed

forbidding

grand

immense

impassable

ingenious

memorable

orchard

pass

sparkle

spectacular

spiral

sturdy

vast

watershed

winding

Writing Task 2

approachable

fall victim to

inevitably

intense

manifold

participate

undisputable

Unit 13

Reading

ambitiously

compound

consequence

endangered

forecast

gain

goods

imbalance

implication

mutually

pour

ratio

reinforce

revenue

sanitation

slim

staggering

stall

surge

surplus

urbanisation

yield

Unit 14

Reading

absolute

afflict

alike

as opposed to

content

convenient

conventional

curious

discipline

distort

fade

flawed

guesswork

implication

inflict

lot

paradox

striking example

tend

undermine

urge

well-being